DecoratinG
PROJECTS

Tricks to transform your home

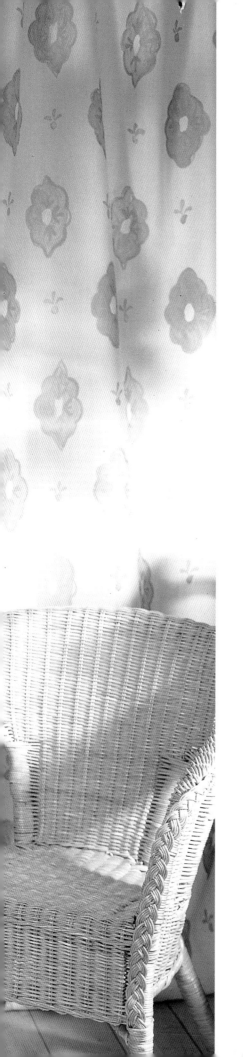

DECORATING
PROJECTS

Tricks to transform your home

Maggie Colvin

hamlyn

DECORATING PROJECTS
Maggie Colvin

First published in Great Britain in 1996 by Hamlyn
an imprint of Octopus Publishing Group Limited
2-4 Heron Quays, London E14 4JP

Reprinted 1997, 1998 (twice)
First published in paperback in 1999

Distributed in the United States by
Sterling Publishing Co, Inc., 387 Park Avenue South,
New York, NY 10016-8810

© Ideal Home, IPC Magazines Ltd 1996
© Additional projects, Maggie Colvin 1996
© Special photography
Octopus Publishing Group Limited 1996

Executive Editor Simon Tuite
Executive Art Editor Mark Stevens
Editor Katie Cowan
Illustration Carol Hill
Photography Di Lewis
Production Mark Walker

A CIP record for this book is available from
the British Library

ISBN 0 600 60109 9

The publishers have made every effort to ensure that
all instructions given in this book are accurate and
safe, but they cannot accept liability for any resulting
injury, damage or loss to either person or property
whether direct or consequential and howsoever
arising. The author and publishers will be grateful for
any information which will assist them in keeping
future editions up to date.

Typset in Adobe Gill Sans Light 46, Adobe Rotis Semi
Serif 9/13 and Adobe Rotis Sans Serif

DESIGNED BY TOWN GROUP CONSULTANCY LIMITED
COLOUR ORIGINATION BY
PICA COLOUR SEPARATION, SINGAPORE
PRODUCED BY TOPPAN PRINTING CO LTD
PRINTED IN CHINA

Contents

Twenty minute tricks

Don't underestimate the effectiveness of these small projects. The simple transformation of a window or an old chair can make a vital visual difference to a room and set the ball rolling. Here are ten quick ideas to inspire you.

Muslin pelmets

If you live on a busy street, or you are overlooked by other houses, it is still possible to create a bit of privacy. These muslin pelmets combined with shutters are a clever way of stopping passers by from staring into your room without blocking sunlight or preventing you from enjoying the skyscape.

TIE ON VOILE PELMET

You will need

Curtain pole to fit your window
Length of striped fabric measuring 3ft (1m)
Length of voile measuring two and a half times the length of the curtain pole
Sewing machine
Needle and thread

This pelmet uses less fabric than the all-in-one swag. You can create a variety of effects by bunching it on the curtain pole in different ways. The swag is made up separately from the tails.

1 With right sides facing, fold the voile in half lengthways and in half again.

2 Cut twelve 1ft 7in x 3in (48 x 8cm) strips of striped fabric, fold in the edges and seam.

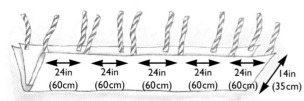

3 Attach the ties to the voile at six equally spaced points along the folded edges, making sure that you sew through all the layers.

4 Tie the voile to the curtain pole to form loose folds.

5 To make the swags, cut the remaining metre of voile into two equal pieces 2ft 9in x 2ft 5 1/2in (88 x 70cm), and cut the bottom of each piece into a semicircular shape and hem the top edge.

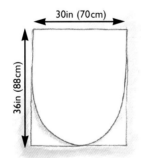

6 Cut 4in (10cm) wide bias binding strips from the remaining striped fabric and seam together enough to edge each swag and allow an extra 2ft (60cm) for the ties.

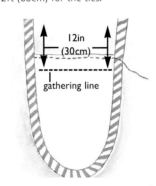

7 With right sides facing, sew the binding strips to the raw edges of the swags, around all the sides except the top edge and leave 1ft (30cm) over at the top of each. Fold the binding twice lengthways to the wrong side and slipstitch in place to create a bound edge. Fold the extended pieces in the same way and oversew the edges. Run a gathering thread along the top of the swag then draw up and tie the end of the thread. Attach the swags to the pole and secure the ties close to the finials.

VOILE SCARF SWAG

To shape the scarf swag fold the voile in two widthways with right sides facing and cut the ends on a 10° diagonal. Topstitch the bobble fringe to the raw side edges and one length of the voile. To secure to the pole, fold the voile in half, push the folded loop over the pole and then thread the ends through the loop to create a knot. To finish scoop the two loose ends over finials of the pole and arrange the tails.

Frosted stencilled window

It was impossible to fit a curtain pole above this corner window that looked out onto a brick wall. This trompe l'oeil roller blind, using stencils and a frosting varnish, produces a delicate imitation etched glass effect and obscures the view while letting in plenty of light.

You will need

Frosting varnish
Stencils
Spray adhesive
Small paint tray or old plate
Fluted architrave to fit your window
Corner blocks
Wooden batten frame

Once you have decided on the overall design, the actual pattern can be rolled on in minutes using a small paint roller and frosting varnish. I centred this design around a laurel wreath, surrounded by a leaf border and edged with a row of tassels that are divided by a blind pull.

Adding a wooden frame made out of fluted architrave with decorative corner block improved the look of the window and enlarged its proportions. To contrast with the terracotta colourwashed walls, I painted the frame and the cupboard doors with grey green emulsion paint that I diluted with water for a colourwash effect. Try rubbing the paint, while still wet, with a rag to create an even finish.

1 Before you begin make sure your window is clean, free from grease and that the glass is dry and not too cold, as any condensation will spoil the result. Cut a piece of paper to the size of your window, plot your design and stencil a trial run.

2 Spray mount your stencil in position, beginning at the centre of the design and working outwards.

3 Pour a small amount of the frosting varnish into the paint tray or old plate. Dip the roller into the varnish and roll off any excess onto a piece of paper kitchen roll.

4 Next, roll the varnish over the stencil to create the frosted effect. Remove the stencil and continue to decorate the remaining window surface, reapplying the stencils and taking care not to touch newly stencilled areas. Once the frosting has dried the glass can be cleaned with soapy water but do not use solvent based window cleaning agents.

5 To create the frame, cut two pieces of fluted architrave to match the height of the window and one for the top edge to fit between the two corner blocks. Paint with the colourwash before securing to the wall with an all purpose adhesive. In the case of uneven walls, you may need to screw a flat wooden batten frame to the plaster using 1 x ¼in (2.5 x 1cm) flat timber to which the fluted architrave and corner pieces can be glued with wood adhesive.

Valentine wreath

For a Valentine's party or a romantic dinner for two, here is a simple idea, using shiny red cardboard and a bunch of flowers, to create a heart shaped table centre.

  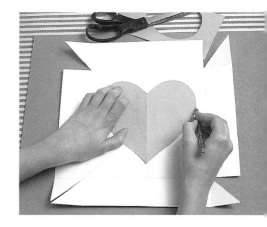

You will need

Flat flower heads – if you want to use roses and tulips, try tweaking the petals back

Several lengths of ivy to wrap around the sides of the lid

Piece of red card, large enough to make a lid to cover the baking tin

Ruler

Pencil

Scissors

Skewer

Glue

Small craft knife

There are plenty of heart shaped biscuit and cake tins on the market but, if you don't happen to own one, any low, flat oval or rectangular dish will do – a roasting dish is ideal. If you have a round flat deep dish, you can try cutting a circle of card to the same size and then simply place it on top of the dish.

1 Measure the outside length, width and height of your container. Turn the card wrong side up and measure and draw this rectangular shape as shown.

2 Using a dotted line draw a second rectangle within the first. Cut along the solid diagonal lines at the corners with scissors and score along the dotted lines with a craft knife, taking care not to cut all the way through the card.

3 Cut out a heart shaped template, to fit the top of the lid, out of old newspaper by folding the paper in half and drawing half a heart shape.

4 Place the cardboard shiny face down and draw around the heart template with a pencil.

5 With the skewer prick holes along the heart shaped pencil line, leaving gaps of about 2in (5cm) between each hole.

6 Fold along the scored lines and glue the triangular tabs to the back of the lid sides to hold the box together.

7 Fill the baking tin with water. Slot the flower heads through the skewered holes and cut the stems to an equal length so their ends dip into the water but they sit flush to the card. Decorate the folded edges of the box with the lengths of ivy, pinning or gluing them in place.

Slotted curtains

Love your French windows but don't know how to dress them without blocking the doorway? These slotted curtains on swing arm rods provide a simple solution to a problem doorway and, depending on the choice of fabric, will adapt to any decorating scheme, from a country style to oriental opulence.

You will need

Fabric to fit the your window
Swing arm curtain rods
Scissors
Needle and thread
Sewing machine

Deciding on a style of curtains for French doors can be a problem. Anything elaborate or bulky may get in the way as you open them, blinds can look stark and hinged shutters are relatively expensive. One of the best solutions is to use a portiere rod. These swing arm curtain rods screw onto the front of the door and swivel to open and close. The curtains simply slot on to the rod so all you need to sew is a simple casing. For those who can't sew, cut the fabric to size, use iron on tape to hide the raw edges, and attach with clip on hooks.

THE COUNTRY LOOK

One of the most effective colour schemes, which always looks fresh and appealing, is blue and white or cream. Worked in simple checks and stripes, set against colourwashed walls in hazy mauve and blue (*see page 139*), the look is truly unbeatable. Furnish the room with basic rus- tic furniture, garden chairs, or a garden bench sofa (*see page 128*) to add to the homely weathered appearance of the walls.

1 Measure from the top of the door to the floor and add 1ft (30cm) for the heading and the bottom hem.

2 Cut the fabric in half length-ways. Turn in each side seam by ½in (1cm) and then ¾in (2cm). Press and machine hem. of both pieces of fabric in by 1in (2.5cm). Then turn under another 5in (12.5cm). Press and tack close to the folded edge.

3 Machine stitch along the line of tacking then make a casing for the rod by stitching a line 2in (5cm) from the first row. Slot the curtain casing onto the swing arm rods.

4 If you don't want to swivel open the curtains, you can also let light in by bunching the middle of the curtain material and holding it in place with an elastic band to create a rosette.

THE OPULENT EASTERN LOOK

An Indian paisley wallpaper teamed with richly patterned brocades, modern black wrought iron furniture, a Moroccan striped rug and ornately framed oil paintings combines a mixture of styles but emphasizes the unifying power of a consistent and sumptuous colour scheme.

Swagged table

For a summer party out of doors, or any special celebration, it is remarkable what a length of white voile swagged around the tablecloth can do for a buffet table, setting an atmosphere of bubbly exuberance and extravagant hospitality.

You will need

*Length of voile, 4ft 6in (1.37cm)
for each 2ft (61cm) wide swag*
Safety pins
*White or light coloured elastic
bands*
Table
Tablecloth

This is an instant decorative treatment intended for a special occasion. As the voile is only held together with elastic bands and pins, when the party is over you can take it apart, wash the

voile and put it back on its cardboard roll which is the best way to keep it free of creases. I have used round table tops, but you can of course recreate the same effect using a rectangular table, positioning the knots at the corners and the middle of the longer sides. You can cut the material in half lengthways to make it go further but bear in mind that the swags will look slightly less opulent.

1 Begin by bunching together one end of the voile and secure this with an elastic band about

8in (20cm) from the cut end. Pin the voile onto the edge of the tablecloth with a safety pin, making sure the pin is tucked out of sight.

2 Standing 2ft (60cm) away from the first elastic band, bunch the fabric again. Holding it firmly in your left hand take a 1ft 4in–1ft 6in (40–46cm) tuck, fold in two and wrap an elastic band over the base to form a secure loop. Then take the end of the loop and push this back into the hole created by the elastic band to form a rosette.

3 Pin the knot or rosette to the tablecloth, making sure the pin is hidden. Open out and shape the folds of the fabric to create a swag. Repeat step 2 in the position of the next rosette.

4 Continue this process until you have worked your way around the entire tablecloth. So that the final end piece sits happily with your first 8in (20cm) tie, cut it to the same length or slightly longer so it gives the appearance of belonging to the same bow.

Chair throws

For a relaxed informal look, the cost of a quilted throw, which gives a shabby chair a facelift, is far less than the price of making fitted covers. To create a stylish variation take an upright chair and wrap it in an exotic fabric with theatrical effect.

You will need

Upright chair with a square seat
Crease resistant fabric measuring 9ft (3m) in length
Strong elastic bands
Bolster cushion about same width as the chair seat
Corded tassel
Pinking shears
Ready made feather filled cushion, the same size as the chair seat
White fabric tape
Safety pins

When your old upholstery has worn out this simple disguise can save a chair that is still structurally sound until the day comes when you are able to afford new covers. The line between securing a throw that will not crumple and fall off as people sit in the chair and still remain easy to remove for washing is a fine one. I unashamedly use safety pins but feel free to substitute these by sewing on Velcro pads which are kinder to flimsy fabrics in the long run.

STYLISH DINING CHAIR COVER

1 Measure the bolster cushion and add 8in (2cm) to the width and an extra 1ft (30cm) to the length.

2 With the pinking shears cut a rectangle of fabric to fit the bolster. Wrap this around the bolster and secure the ends with elastic bands, trim with the corded tassel and then splay the ends to make a party cracker shape.

3 Cut the tape into 1½ft lengths. Fold each length in two and sew the folded end firmly to each of the four corners of the cushion. Tie the tapes under the legs of the chair seat to hold the cushion in place.

4 Place the rest of the fabric over the chair seat and back. Make a 6in (15cm) fold at the front edge so it lines up with the floor. This overhang will eventually be picked up by elastic bands.

5 Smooth the fabric over the seat and tuck it under the back of the cushion. Use two safety pins or Velcro pads to secure the fabric to the cushion.

6 Pull the remaining the fabric over the back of the chair. Turn the chair back to face you and gather the excess fabric from into one central rosette, securing it firmly with the elastic bands.

7 Make two more bunches, following Step 6, in line with the front corners of the chair seat. Round off the square corners of the fabric with the pinking shears in long gentle curves. Cut straight across the bottom, front and back of the fabric to give the cover a consistent serrated edge.

ARMCHAIR THROW

To create this less formal arm-chair cover, match the length-ways centre line of the bed-spread with the centre line of the chair. Lay the bedspread over the chair making sure that end sits just above floor level. Smooth it over the chair seat, pushing the cover into the gaps around the seat, and continue over the back of the chair tucking more fabric into the gaps. It is important to do this firmly as it helps keep the throw looking tidier for longer when in use. To lift the bedspread off the floor behind the chair, bunch the fabric and secure with elastic bands to make two large rosettes.

Over the pole curtains

For the non-sewing brigade, this window treatment is heaven sent. You can create a variety of different effects using three lengths of fabric, slotted over a pole and arranged in a pattern of overlapping swags.

You will need

Voile to fit the length
of your window
Curtain pole
Silk neck scarves
Pinking shears

Not only are these curtains speedy to make, they are also easy to remove for washing, so you can justify treating yourself to a white translucent fabric that filters a soft serene light similar to the effect produced by Japanese screens. For the ties I used silk neck scarves and then experimented with the different shapes you can create by tying two back curtains across a front curtain in bunches or with a loose tie. With the six lengths shown here the potential for different swags and groupings is endless.

1 To work out how much material you need, double your pole-to-floor measurement and add 6in (15cm). Cut the number of lengths you require with the pinking shears.

2 Fold each length of fabric in half and arrange them right side up, over the pole to make six lengths. Each piece should be evenly gathered and take up an equal amount of space.

3 Bunch the right- and left-handed sections a little over half way down the curtain length and secure behind a fixed curtain tie or with silk scarves.

4 The centre four lengths can be bunched together, tied as shown in the photographs or gathered in any way that looks pleasing to you.

Decoupage lampshade and wastepaper basket

Black paint is a brilliantly easy way to hide stains on old card lampshades and wastepaper baskets. It provides the perfect background to these delightful decoupage cherubs, creating stylish matching accessories.

You will need

Black enamel paint
Small paintbrush
Adhesive spray or PVA glue
Small pair of scissors
Acrylic varnish

A few distinguished accessories will liven up a monotone interior and this lampshade and decoupage will make a stylish addition to any room. The photocopier has enormously helped keep the cost of glamour in check.

1 Clean the lamp shade with a damp cloth and wipe dry. Paint the shade with one coat of the black paint and leave to dry.

2 Photocopy the cherubs on a good quality machine and cut them out with the small scissors. Experiment with different looks by placing them in different positions, using short bursts of adhesive spray, until you find a composition you are pleased with.

3 Apply a proper amount of spray mount to the cut outs, stick them firmly in place and, working from the centre out-wards, smooth them down.

4 Apply clear varnish. Three or four coats is recommended although the decoupage experts will tell you the more you apply, the better the results. If you want an antiqued look you can add a tiny bit of yellow oil paint to the varnish.

5 Apply the same technique to the wastepaper basket.

Swagged bedhead

A softly draped frothy swag in pure white voile may be all you need to show off a bed to stunning effect in a room lined with a busy patterned wallcovering.

above the top of the mattress and centred over the bed. The other two hooks should be 3ft (1m) above the top of the mattress, in line with each outer edge of the bed.

2 Find the centre of voile, by folding it in half widthways. Sew gathering stitches along the centre line in white thread, stopping 1ft 8in (50cm) from the edge.

3 Mark two more lines 3ft (1m) from each end of the fabric and sew a gathering thread along each line in the same way. Hem the raw edges.

4 Gather all three threads tightly and knot them.

5 Tie the gold cord which is attached to the angels around the three bunches of fabric. Place the angels on the picture hooks and arrange the fabric folds.

You will need

*Plain white voile measuring
   5ft (5m) in length
Three angel picture hooks
Sewing machine
Gold tasselled cord
Scissors
Needle and thread*

This has to be one of the quickest, simplest bedhead treatments, using just three decorative gilt Renaissance style cherub head picture hooks to form a triangle that spans the width of a double bed. The secret is to gather only one third of the width of the voile, which gives the swag a deep flowing frill, and falls into a softly draped centre piece that falls like a wedding train.

1 Position and nail the hooks to form a triangle above the bedhead. The middle hook looks best positioned about 5ft (1.5m)

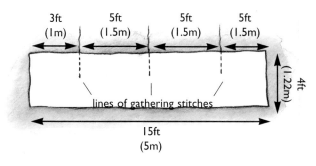

Ribboned baskets

For anyone who collects baskets and loves ribbons, here is a pretty way to combine the two. Filled with fruit, plants, bath salts, cookies, chocolates or jams, they make practical and beautiful presents, in containers too good to throw away.

 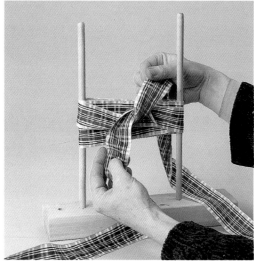 

You will need

Small wicker basket with handle
Ribbon measuring
   1in x 4ft 6in (2.5cm x 1.5m)
Double sided tape
Spray of silk or dried flowers
Florists' wire, two lengths
   measuring 6in (15 cm)
Wire cutters
Bow maker
Scissors

If you don't have a bow maker it is very easy to make your own with a piece of planed softwood 2 ¹/₂in (6.5cm) wide x 1 ¹/₂ (4cm) high x 8in (20cm) long. Drill several ¹/₂in (1cm) holes spaced at 1in (2.5cm) intervals along the piece of wood to allow you to make different sized bows. Then push two 1 x 9in (2.5 x 25cm) dowels into the holes. Move the dowels further apart to make a larger bow and closer together to make a smaller bow.

1 Secure one end of the ribbon to the basket handle using a short strip of double sided tape. Wind the ribbon back round and over it to hide and secure this end. Continue winding the ribbon round the handle. When you have completely covered the handle, tie a simple knot to secure the ribbon. Cut the ribbon about 2in (5cm) from the knot at an angle. This extra length will help to keep the ribbon from slipping and will eventually appear to be part of the decorative bow.

2 Make two bows with the rest of the ribbon. Begin by winding the ribbon around the bow maker two or three times, depending on how full a bow you want and how much ribbon you have left.

3 Tie the ribbon around the loops in a firm knot exactly in the middle of the bow. Lift it free of the wooden uprights and splay the loops out at each end. Cut the ribbon ends off at an angle. Make a second bow.

4 Make up two small bunches of silk of dried flowers. You may need to use wire cutters to cut the silk flowers. Wrap them securely with florists' wire. Pass another piece of wire through the back of the loop of one of the bows and twist one end around a posy. Then twist both ends of wire around the base of the handle to secure the bow and flowers to the basket. Repeat on the other side of the basket.

5 Fill the basket with potted flowers and fruit, or use it as a pretty container in the bathroom.

Forty minute feats

Improvisation often yields unexpectedly successful results; an old branch for the trunk of a topiary tree or bedspreads for curtains will look dazzlingly original. Tracking down inexpensive fabrics and treating them royally with goblet headings and Italian stringing is another reliable thrifty decorator's trick. Finally, for a magical way to revive wooden furniture, this dyeing and liming technique works wonders without obscuring the beauty of the wood's natural grain.

Topiary tree

This is one of those elegant sophisticated accessories you long to buy from smart flower shops — you can, of course, make one yourself at a fraction of the cost. If you can find an old branch to use instead of the wooden dowelling, the topiary tree will look more natural and cost even less.

You will need

Red satin ribbon measuring
   1½in x 3ft (4cm x 1m)
Wooden dowelling measuring
   1in x 1ft 5in (2.5cm x 43cm)
Spangled bead chain measuring
   3ft (1m)
Patterned or plain terracotta
   flowerpot
Adhesive tape
Strong waterproof tape
Small packet of cellulose filler
Oasis ball, 6in (15cm) in diameter
Real or artificial holly
Florists' wire
Nine fir cones
Dried moss

Tartan wired ribbon measuring
   3ft (1m)
Scissors
Skewer or pencil

WINTER TREE

Once you have made the basic structure, namely a piece of wooden dowelling embedded in a pot of filler topped with a ball of oasis, you can dress this tree up for winter and restyle it for spring. In the summer you can soak the oasis in water and decorate it with fresh summer flowers and, at Christmas try a combination of dried rose heads, white lavender, fir cones and holly.

1 Wind the red satin ribbon around the dowelling, securing both ends with a piece of adhesive tape. Repeat with the spangled bead chain.

2 Cover the hole at the bottom of the flowerpot with the strong waterproof tape. Following the instructions on the packet mix enough cellulose filler to fill the flowerpot to about 1in (2.5cm) below the top.

3 Using a skewer or pencil, pierce a small hole about 2in (5cm) deep in the oasis and push the wooden doweling into the same spot. Push the other end of the doweling into the filler in an upright position and remove the oasis. Allow the filler to set for about an hour.

4 Replace the oasis and then insert the sprigs of holly at even spaces making sure that the surface of the ball is completely hidden. Attach a wire stem to each fir cone and position them evenly amongst the holly.

5 Finally, cover the exposed filler with moss and tie a bow around the base of the tree's stem.

SUMMER TREE

If you prefer the dried roses idea
you will need most of the materials listed above but for the holly
and fir cones substitute forty dried
roses and six white lavender
sprays. Twist a second piece of
ribbon around the dowelling
instead of the spangled bead
chain. Cut the rose heads, leaving
a 1in (2.5cm) stem on each, snip
the lavender heads so they are
2in (5cm) long and arrange as
before. Cover the filler with moss
and a few extra roses, and finish
with a bow.

Bedspread curtains

For those who cannot sew, dislike sewing, or cannot afford the expense of having curtains made, this is my favourite short cut to curtains, using two cream bedspreads and tassel tiebacks.

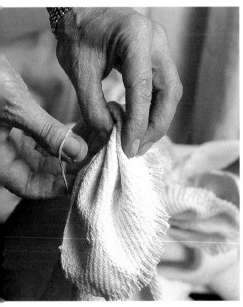
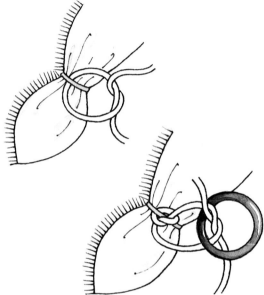

You will need

*Two bedspreads, single or double,
  to fit your windows*
Elastic bands
*White fabric tape measuring
  9ft (3m) in length*
*Four 3ft (1m) long cords with
  tassels on each end*
Curtain pole
Curtain rings
Two fleur-de-lys tiebacks

There are several different ways to dress curtains without having to get out the sewing machine. The key is to chose ready hemmed fabrics like bedspreads, shawls, travel rugs, scarves - even saris - as opposed to fabric sold by the yard or metre.

1 Fold each bedspread in half widthways and then in half again. Mark the top of each fold with a pin.

2 Bunch the fabric at each end of the bedspread and then again at the three marked points to form 3in (7.5cm) peaks. Secure with the elastic bands.

3 Cut the white tape into five 6in (15cm) lengths and thread one piece through the back of each elastic band. Knot the white tape around the elastic bands and tie each tape securely around a curtain ring.

4 Working at the front of the curtain, make a simple knot around each bunch of fabric with the tasselled cord. Leave a generous length of cord to fall between each bunch and allow the tasselled ends to hang down at either side of the curtain.

5 Tie a second tasselled cord to the outermost bunch of the curtain so that the tassels hang down the outside edge.

6 Repeat Steps 1–5 for the second curtain. Fix the tiebacks in place and arrange the curtains behind them.

Formal window treatments

This fan shaped blind is one of my favourite window treatments and always looks stunningly impressive. I have also included Italian stringing which, depending on the fabric you use, is easily adaptable to both modern and traditional interiors.

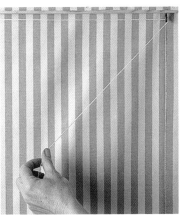

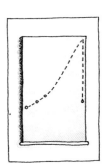

You will need

Fabric cut to fit the window recess. Add 1in (2.5cm) for side turnings and 3in (7.5cm) to the length

Roman blind tape the same length as the fabric

Wooden batten measuring 1 x 1in (2.5 x 2.5cm), as long as the width of your window

Two 1in (2.5cm) screw eye hooks

Cleat

Curtain cord measuring 9ft (3m)

FAN BLIND

The curtains are made up in a cream moire, interlined with goblet headings and pulled open by Italian stringing. You can buy ready made tape, with fixed position hooks, that attach the curtains to screw eyes mounted on the curved pelmet board cut from Medium Density Fibreboard (MDF). The pelmet is fixed above the window on angle brackets. You need one screw eye for each goblet, evenly spaced to line up with the position of the hooks.

1 Cut out the fabric and make two ¹/₂ in (1cm) turns down both sides and hem or topstitch. Repeat for the top edge. Turn up the bottom edge taking up the hem allowance in two folds.

2 Working from the right side, mark the lengthways centre of the blind with a row of pins. Place the Roman blind tape in the centre on the wrong side, positioning it over the pin line and tacking in place. Remove pins. Seam the tape in place down both long side edges.

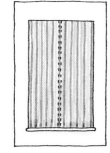

3 Wrap the top of the blind around the batten and staple in place. Screw one eye hook to the middle of the batten above the tape and another one at the righthand end of the batten.

4 Thread the curtain cord through the Roman blind tape. Knot it on the bottom loop and thread it through the eye hooks.

5 Screw to batten to the top of the window recess. Fix the cleat to one side of the frame at a halfway position. Pull up the cord to form a fan shape. Hold in position by securing the cord to the cleat.

ITALIAN STRINGING

Pale plain fabrics are suited to this cording that runs along the back of the curtains through small brass rings. Sew the rings in a diagonal line starting

2ft (60cm) below the top of the curtain to 6in (15cm) below the opposite top corner. Tie a length of blind cord to the lowest brass ring positioned on the centre edge and thread it through the remaining hooks. Lever through a screw eye attached to the pelmet board at the top corner and secure on a cleat screwed halfway down the window frame.

Coronet bedhead

For a soft romantic bedroom look translucent muslin, draped from a coronet encircled with ivy, sets a fairy tale scene in this cottage style bedroom, in which the curtains appear to be held back by hovering doves.

You will need

Two widths of fabric to line the
*   back wall*
Two widths of fabric for the side
*   curtains*
Artificial ivy
Blue checked ribbon measuring
*   6ft (2m) in length*
Tracing paper
White paper painted pale blue
Scissors
Simple brass hooks
White fabric tape
All purpose glue
Acrylic varnish
Needle and thread

A white on white colour scheme, with bedlinen introducing a blue bow motif, evokes an atmosphere of country freshness. The coronet is a semicircular track which screws to the wall about 5ft (1.5m) above the bed, but the exact position should be determined by the height of the ceiling. You will probably need about 24ft (8m) of fabric for the side curtains but this will depend on the height of your ceiling.

1 Sew the widths of curtain fabric together lengthways. Turn over the top raw edge and pin, tack and seam the gathering tape to the inside edge.

2 Hook the curtains in place and surround the top with the artificial ivy which should be slip-stitched at 1ft (30cm) intervals.

3 Trace the bird pattern printed here, enlarge it on a photocopier and cut it out. Next, place it on

the sheet of painted paper and cut around the shape. Reverse the pattern so that the bird faces in the opposite direction and cut out the second bird shape.

4 Screw the brass hooks in position on the wall so that they are clear of the mattress' edge and in line with the tops of the pillows. Sew a small loop of fabric tape to each of the outside edges, 4ft 2in (1.27m) from the top edge of the curtain, and slip them over the brass hooks to hold the curtains in place.

5 Position the doves on the wall, with their beaks facing the brass hooks. Glue them in place and apply two coats of varnish for as a protective coating.

6 Cut the blue checked ribbon in half. Tie two bows, sew the centre of each bow to the base of a loop and arrange neatly.

Dyed and limed table

Once the layers of treacly varnish had been removed from this oak table, its decorative potential was easier to spot. An attractive grain, decorative side and front panels, and turned legs took naturally to this blue grey dye and white liming effect, which compliments the blue room it was destined for, without obliterating the grain.

You will need

Copper wire brush
Blue grey wood dye
Fine grade steel wool
Liming wax
Neutral wax furniture polish
Two soft cotton rags
Acrylic varnish

Liming must be carried out on bare wood, so I delivered this table to my local paint stripping firm, although it is cheaper of course to do it yourself. Once you have stripped the table, the idea is to remove some of the wood pulp and allow the dye and lime to stick in the crevices. You can also use a paint colour (emulsion) instead of the liming wax and dye.

1 Brush hard in the direction of the wood grain with the copper wire brush to remove some of the soft pulp. Wipe or blow away the wood dust.

2 Apply the wood dye lightly with a rag and wipe off any excess so that the wood grain shows through.

3 Using the steel wool rub on the liming wax. Leave to dry for ten minutes.

4 Dip a fresh piece of steel wool into the polish and rub over the surface to remove some of the liming wax

5 Finally, polish the table, using a clean cotton rag. This gives a soft lustrous sheen to the muted grey blue wood grain finish.

6 To protect, apply a coat of acrylic varnish.

One hour workovers

*I find the challenge of making
something beautiful out of cheap mass
produced furniture irresistible. This
chapter is about adding style and
distinction to unwanted furniture in
simple ways, using wooden mouldings,
stencils, paint and fabric. It includes my
most recent favourite discovery, how to
recycle shabby lampshades, and an old
favourite, the way to avoid corner
seams when making chair covers.*

Bookcase revamp

Any mass produced bookcase can be improved by a few distinguished mouldings and imaginative additions; a calico blind, some tartan ribbons and a tartan wrapping paper backing. The difference is remarkable and easy to achieve.

You will need

Woodwash (or emulsion paint)
Paintbrush
Staple gun or hammer and tacks
Tartan wrapping paper
Tartan ribbon or braid
Calico
Dressmaker's pins
All purpose glue
Wooden batten 1 x ½in (2.5 x 1cm)
  and cut to the width of
  the bookcase
Panel pins
Wood glue
Moulding
Sewing machine
Needle and thread

For this transformation the choice of moulding is vital. It needs a generously wide and fluted design with classical style corner pieces of the same size to obscure the rather average proportions of this utilitarian shape.

1 Cut wrapping paper to fit each section of the bookcase back and glue in place. Next cut ribbon or braid to fit along each shelf edge and glue in position.

2 Measure and cut a piece of calico to the height and width of the bookcase. Remember to subtract the width of the mouldings

but add 1½in (3cm) to the width and 4in (10cm) to the length for the hems.

3 Turn back and machine a ½in (1.5cm) side hem along the length of the blind. Make a ½in (1.5cm) hem along the wrong side of the bottom edge of the blind, add a 2in (5cm) turning and machine stitch to make a casing for the batten.

4 Cut two pieces of tartan ribbon twice the height of the bookcase. Fold the ribbon in half and position each length over the top edge of the blind so that it hangs down the back and the front. Make sure the two lengths of ribbon are placed at an equal distance, 6in (15cm), from the sides and pin in place.

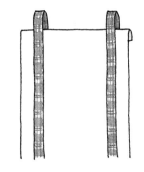

5 Cut the moulding into three pieces, two for the sides and one for the top, to fit between corner pieces. Put one tablespoon of

woodwash in a saucer and dilute with one tablespoon of water. Brush this mixture lightly over the mouldings and corner pieces, so that the grain still shows, and leave to dry.

6 Using panel pins and wood glue, secure the side mouldings in place so they sit flush with the outer edge of the bookcase.

7 Staple or tack the top front edge of the blind to the bottom back edge of the top moulding, taking care to remove the pins holding the ribbons and secure the ribbons with the staple gun or tacks. Cut the batten to the width of the blind and slot through the blind casing.

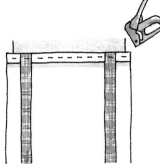

8 Turn the moulding the right way round and glue and tack it in position. It should sit flush with the top of the bookcase and leave enough space on either side for the corner pieces. Position, glue and tack corner pieces in place. Roll up the blind to the desired height and tie the ribbons to hold in place, making sure the batten is straight.

Antiqued decorated drinks table

By using a favourite curtain fabric as the pattern for a stencil in terracotta and gilt,
this ordinary reproduction table was turned into a beautiful occasional table.

You will need

Black emulsion paint
Terracotta emulsion paint
Pot of gilt cream
Stencil brush
Household brush
Large sheet of acetate
Tracing paper
Felt tip pen
Hot pen
Spray mount
Masking tape
Piece of glass to fit your stencil design
Clear acrylic gloss varnish

This mahogany table started life as part of a nest of three, but it had so many stains and dents that it really was not worth restoring the wood. Before painting it, I filled the holes with a wood filler and sandpapered it to a smooth finish. If you don't have a hot knife you can always use a shop bought stencil.

1 Apply the base coat colour and leave to dry.

2 Make the stencil by tracing the fabric design. If you can find a stencilled fabric design it makes the job easier. Lay the fabric flat, then firmly secure the tracing paper on top with the masking tape. Trace the outline of the design leaving bridges as necessary to define and separate the shapes in a stencil design.

3 Place the tracing paper under the glass and position the acetate on top. Draw around the design with the hot knife. Most of the cut out pieces will fall away easily but cut off any that stick with scissors.

4 Place the stencil over the table top, secure with masking tape, and stencil with the terracotta paint.

5 While this is drying apply the gilt cream to the table top edges. Apply a rope design stencil in terracotta to the top and bottom braces of the table and to the legs. Leave to dry.

6 For the gilt cream stencil coat, set the stencil slightly off register so that the terracotta will show around some edges. Apply lightly to create a slightly patchy effect.

7 Leave to dry overnight before applying two coats of varnish.

Dining chair cover

Metal framed chairs can look dazzlingly decorative on a hot summer's day but they are often cold and uncomfortable to sit on. Here is a wrap-over cover that will convert a metal seat into comfortable a dining chair. It is designed to be easy to sew as all the complicated joins are tied.

You will need

Wooden or metal chair with arms
Wide fabric 12ft x 3ft 6in (4 x1.2m)
Lightweight terrylene wadding
measuring 12 ft x3ft 6in
(4 x 1.2m)
White fabric tape
Cushion pad, slightly smaller than
the chair seat
Brown paper
Pencil
Large knitting needle
Sewing machine
Needle and thread

This cover is made from three separate pieces. The pattern is shaped for a gothic style back but can easily be adapted. Even a kitchen chair can be given the same treatment. The terrylene interlining is crucial, as it will soften the metal and make the fabric look more expensive.

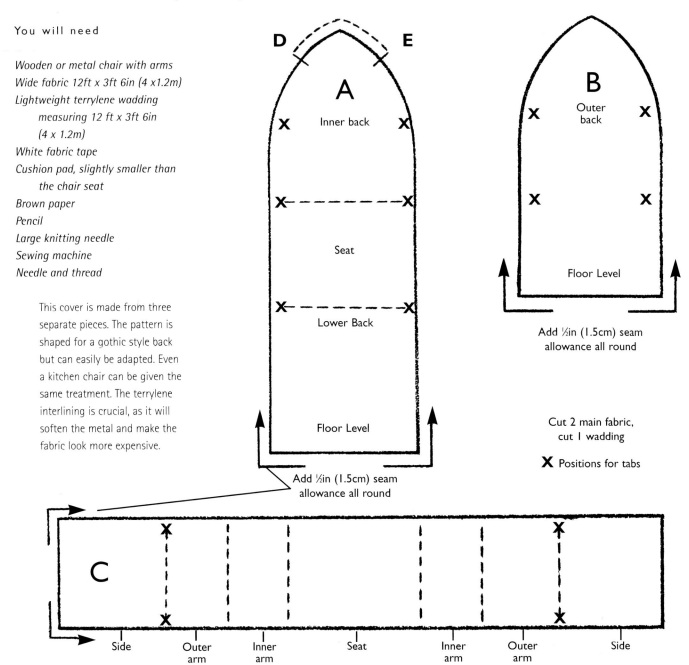

A Inner back
Seat
Lower Back
Floor Level
D **E**

Add ½in (1.5cm) seam allowance all round

B Outer back
Floor Level

Add ½in (1.5cm) seam allowance all round

Cut 2 main fabric, cut 1 wadding

X Positions for tabs

C
Side Outer arm Inner arm Seat Inner arm Outer arm Side

1 Start by tracing the shape of the chair back, from the highest point down to seat level, onto the brown paper. Cut out the shape to make a template.

2 Measure the width and depth of the seat, the height of the seat from the ground and the height and depth of the arms. Using the template and these measurements, take your fabric and cut out shapes A, B and C twice, adding a 1/2in (1.5cm) seam allowance all round.

3 Cut out shapes A,B and C in wadding. Shape A will cover the front of the chair from the top of the inner back to the floor level. Shape B will be a straight piece covering the back of the chair.

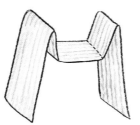

Shape C will cover the arms and the seat of the chair down to floor.

4 To make the ties, cut out 14 strips of fabric, 2 1/2 x 9in (6.5 x 23 cm). Fold each in half lengthways with right sides facing. Sew around the edges, leaving one end open and allowing a 1/2in (1cm) seam. Clip corners, trim seam allowances and turn right sides out, poking the corners out carefully with a large knitting needle. Press.

5 Pin a tie to the right side of one of each pair of pieces A, B, C at the points marked with a cross, raw edges level and the tie pointing inwards towards the centre of the piece. Tack the ties in place close to the seam line. Place the wadding on the wrong side of the other piece of the fabric of each pair and tack close

to the seam allowance with large stitches.

6 With right sides facing, sew the seams of each pair of the three main pieces A, B and C together around all the edges, leaving a big enough gap to turn the pieces. Trim wadding and seams, and clip curves where necessary; turn right sides out through the opening. Slipstitch openings and press.

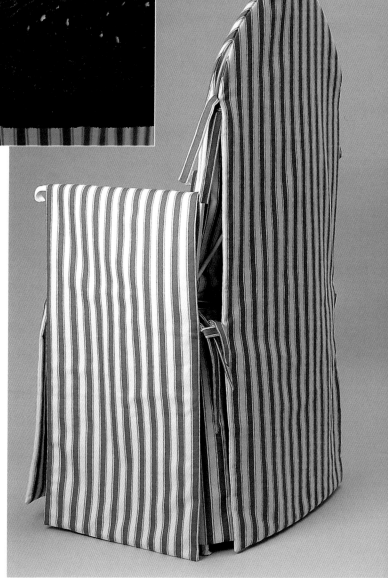

7 Measure the height of the seat from the ground and, multiplying this by 6in (15cm), cut out eight kick pleats from the fabric adding ½in (1.5cm) all round for turnings. These kick pleats will cover the chair legs. For the pleat on the first leg, take two pieces and sew round all edges with right sides facing, leaving an opening for turning. Turn the pleat right way out, press and sew two 6in (5cm) lengths of fabric tape to both top corners.

8 Tie the kick pleats to the seat frame to cover the chair legs as shown. If the chair has a solid wooden seat fix medium sized screw eyes to the underside of the seat in the appropriate places and tie the pleats on to

these. Repeat for the other legs.

9 Place the pieces A, B and C in position on the chair as shown, putting piece C in place first. Place the cushion pad between pieces A and C. Knot the ties together. In some places you will be tying more than one pair together. Finally, slipstitch pieces A and B together at the top, between points D and E as marked on pattern A.

Revamps for lamps

When a lampshade begins to look grubby, or a light bulb leaves a burn mark, don't throw it away. Making your own lampshades to tie in with the style of your room is rewarding, and a coat of paint can give an old shade a new lease of life. The key to successful lampshade painting is to apply at least two coats of paint so that when the lamp is on the brush marks will not show. Once the second coat of paint is dry, the decorative possibilities are endless.

**STAR STAMPED
LAMPSHADE**

You will need

White emulsion paint
Mid-blue acrylic paint
Clear acrylic glaze
Star stamp measuring 3in (7.5cm)
Small paintbrush
Comb
Clear acrylic varnish

I combed this lamp with a blue glaze and stamped a row of stars along the bottom edge to coordinate with the star and trellis base I already had at home.

1 First paint the lampshade in two coats of the white paint.

2 Mix one large tablespoonful of the blue paint with the acrylic glaze and brush a generous coating onto the lampshade with even strokes.

3 Starting on the top back seam of the shade, drag the comb around the surface of the lampshade in a horizontal line until the shade is covered in an even texture. If you make a mistake, or you want to improve your combing lines, you can brush out the combed effect and start again.

4 While the glaze is still wet, press the stamp along the base of the shade to make a straight line of stars.

5 When the glaze is dry, apply a protective coat of acrylic varnish.

STRIPED SHADE

You will need

Yellow emulsion paint
Tinted acrylic glaze
Comb
Mutton cloth or loose weave
  cotton fabric
Small paintbrush
Tape measure
Clear acrylic varnish

A simple and most effective striped finish can be created by running a finger covered with mutton cloth down a shade coated in paint and glaze. The soft pale yellow and green colours I chose for this shade contrasted with the black wrought iron lamp base I already had at home.

1 Apply two coats of yellow emulsion and leave to dry.

2 Divide the top circumference of the shade into even spaces. For this shade I have used ½in (1cm) gaps. Mark these lightly in pencil inside the top of the rim.

3 Paint the shade with the tinted glaze and comb from top to bottom creating vertical lines.

4 While the glaze is still wet, cover your index finger with the mutton cloth and drag it through the glaze from the top rim, staring from each pencil mark, to the bottom rim in a straight line.

5 Complete the stripes, which should fan out towards the bottom edge.

6 When the shade is dry apply a protective coat of acrylic varnish.

PIERCED STAR SHADE

You will need

Midnight blue emulsion paint
Star stencil
Tapestry or darning needle
Pencil or felt tip pen
Small paintbrush

Pierced decoration on a shade painted in dark colours can look stunning, especially if you use well defined shapes like this star.

1 Begin by painting the shade with two coats of the midnight blue emulsion paint.

2 Using the star stencil as a template, trace the pattern on the inside of the shade. Reposition and repeat until the shade is evenly decorated.

3 Pierce along the drawn lines with the darning needle, and leaving as little space between the dots as possible, until you have completed the entire shade.

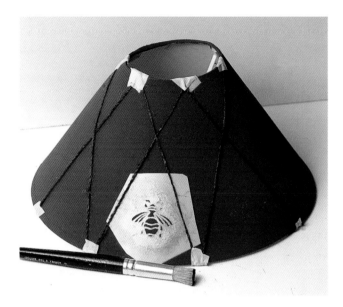

STENCILLED LAMPSHADE

You will need

Terracotta emulsion paint
Gilt cream
Stencil
Acrylic varnish
Spray adhesive
Small paintbrush
Masking tape
Pencil
String
Scissors

A stencilled lampshade can look remarkably smart if you paint it in a classic colour combination. I painted this shade in terracotta and gold to coordinate with the colour scheme and striking heraldic print I already had in the room.

1 Paint the shade with two coats of terracotta emulsion and allow it to dry.

2 Divide the circumference of both the top and the bottom rim into the same number of even spaces and make tiny vertically aligned pencil marks on the inside edge of both rims. Secure a piece of string with masking tape at each pencil mark along the top rim of the shade. Work your way round the lampshade, crossing each piece of string over its neighbour and attaching it at a diagonal slant to the next space along the bottom rim of the shade until you have covered the shade with an evenly spaced diamond and triangular framework.

3 Use spray adhesive to secure the bee stencil firmly in the spaces and stencil with the gilt cream.

4 Leave to dry overnight and finish with a coat of varnish.

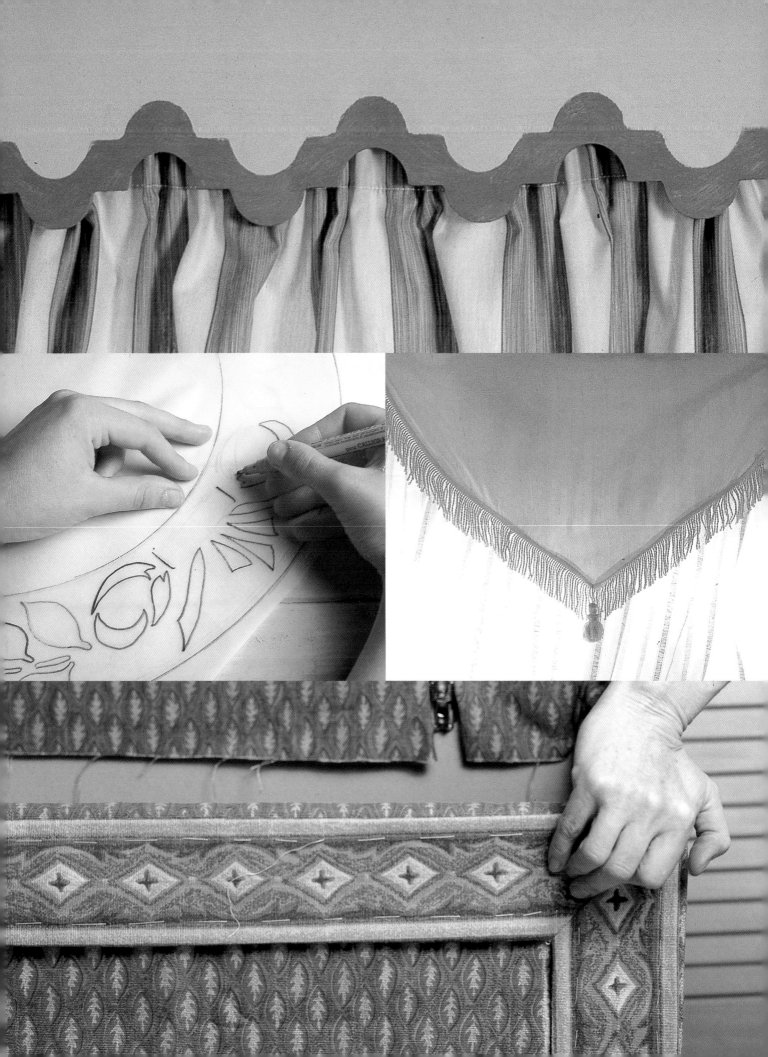

Two hour transformations

Most people decorate a home over a long period, which is fine, because often the decision as to how you tackle one problem in a room provides the impetus to revitalise the whole scheme. Here are eight decorating projects which could provide that vital visual start up. Each is key to a very different look.

Tab headed pelmet

Tall windows often look best with some kind of headed finishing touch. In a modern setting, where traditional swags and tails might look over the top, this less formal tab heading sets a lighter tone and is extremely easy to make.

You will need

Curtain pole
White silk
White lining fabric
Long off-white fringe
Three long white tassels

I chose a luscious combination of sheer curtains and off-white silk to create a breezy summer feel for this pelmet but different fabric combinations will of course create a variety of looks.

1 Adapting the pattern to fit your window, cut three petal shape pieces out of the silk and lining, following the solid lines of the pattern below.

2 With right sides facing, place each piece of silk on top of a piece of lining fabric and sew a ¹/₂in (1cm) seam along the curved edges of each of the three petal shapes. Clip the seam allowances to allow for turnings, being careful not to clip through the stitching, and trim off the pointed end close to the stitching as shown.

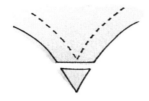

3 Turn the petal shapes right side out, carefully poke out the points and press.

4 Pin and tack the fringing to the front edges of the pelmet and slipstitch in place. Turn in the remaining top raw edges of the pelmet ¹/₂in (1.5cm) to the wrong side of the pelmet and press in place. Tack through all the thicknesses.

5 Cut four pieces of silk measuring 8 x 9in (20 x 23cm) for each of the tabs. With right sides facing sew down the longest edge, allowing for a ¹/₂in (1cm) seam. Turn the right way out and press. Tuck the raw edges in onto each other down the end of the tube and sew the ends together.

6 Lay out the three petal shapes in a row so that the two top corners of the middle piece slightly overlap the two side pieces and pin them in place.

7 Pin a tab to the back of each of these joins. Then pin the remaining two tabs exactly half way along the top edge of the two outer pieces. Tack the tabs in place and then topstitch along the top of the pelmet to join the tabs to the main sections.

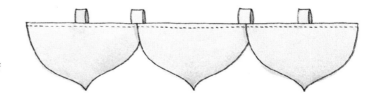

8 Hand sew the three tassels in place and slot the pelmet onto the pole. Place a quarter of the curtain rings between the first two tabs, half of them between the next two tabs and the remaining curtain rings before the final tab. The outer edges of the pelmet will hang down to form swags.

9 Make up simple voile curtains to fit the window and attach them to the curtain rings. If you want working curtains that open and close you should attach them to a track tucked away neatly behind the pole.

Upholstered blanket box

This upholstered blanket box, made from a plain box chest, is ideal for use as a laundry basket in the bathroom or for stashing away winter blankets in the bedroom.

You will need

Box chest with lid made of MDF (Medium Density Fibreboard) or cheap pine
Striped fabric measuring 6ft (2m)
Coordinating printed fabric measuring 6ft (2m)
Lining fabric measuring 9ft (3m)
Medium weight Terylene wadding to fit the box lid
Braid measuring 15ft (4.5m)
Long metal ruler
Dressmaker's pins
Tailor's chalk
Pencil
All purpose glue
Staple gun
Sewing machine
Needle and thread

To cover this box I used two coordinating fabrics, a stripe to frame the shape and a geometric print for the panels and the lid. If you use an old box make sure that it is clean, dry and free of nails.

1 Measure the front and one side panel of the base of the box and, allowing 6in (15cm) for turnings, cut two pieces of the print fabric to this size. Join both with a ½in (1.5cm) seam at the selvedge. Wrap the fabric around the box, wrong side out and pin a second seam to make a close fitting cover. Sew the seam and then trim to ½in (1.5cm).

2 To make the striped frame, cut nine, wide strips of the coordinating striped fabric, enough to make a neat, bold frame on the front and side panels of the box and allowing 1½in (4cm) for turnings all round. To frame the front panel, make a square three sided frame from strips with mitred corners. To form the mitred corners, fold the fabric back on itself, creating a 45° angle, pin and then topstitch. Fold in all the raw edges and press neatly in place.

3 Slip the main cover over the blanket box, carefully positioning the seams on the corners, and, with the tailor's chalk and the metal ruler, mark the corner lines and top edges of the frame to show exactly how it will be positioned.

4 Remove the main cover, pin and tack the frame into position and, using the sewing machine, firmly topstitch the frame in place. Repeat for the side panels.

5 Cut a piece of wadding to fit the box lid and stick in place. Now cut a piece of the patterned fabric to fit the lid, with an allowance of 4in (10cm) on each side. Make up a frame with the striped fabric for the lid, as for Steps 2, 3 and 4, and stretch the completed cover over the lid. Tuck the corners in neatly and staple in position on the underside of the lid.

6 Cut a long strip of fabric to encircle the base of the box. If you have to join strips, try to position the seams in line with the corners. Wrap the strip around the base, stretch and staple the raw edges to the underside and top inside edge of the base.

7 Cut the lining fabric to fit the bottom, lid and all four sides of the box, with a turning allowance of 1in (2.5cm) on each edge. With right sides facing sew together to make up the box shape. Turn in the top raw edges and staple the lining to the top inside edge of the box. Turn in the raw edges, press firmly in place and staple the lining to the underside of the lid.

8 Cover the staples by gluing one line of braid along the underside edges of the lid and another around the inside top edges of the blanket box.

Kitchen chair

A full set of smart dining chairs can set you back a small fortune but, if you can manage to find six structurally sound second hand kitchen chairs of roughly the same shape and size, new fabric covers can transform them beyond all recognition.

You will need

Length of print fabric measuring
9ft x 4ft 4in (2.74 x1.32m)
Length of coordinating plain glazed
cotton measuring
4ft 4in x 3ft (1.2m x 91cm)
Cushions to pad the frame
Piping cord
Bias binding to match the
glazed cotton
White fabric tape
Scissors
Staple gun
Brown paper
Measuring tape
Sewing machine
Needle and thread

A – height of back from seat
B – width of back
C – height of seat from ground
D – depth of seat
E – width of seat

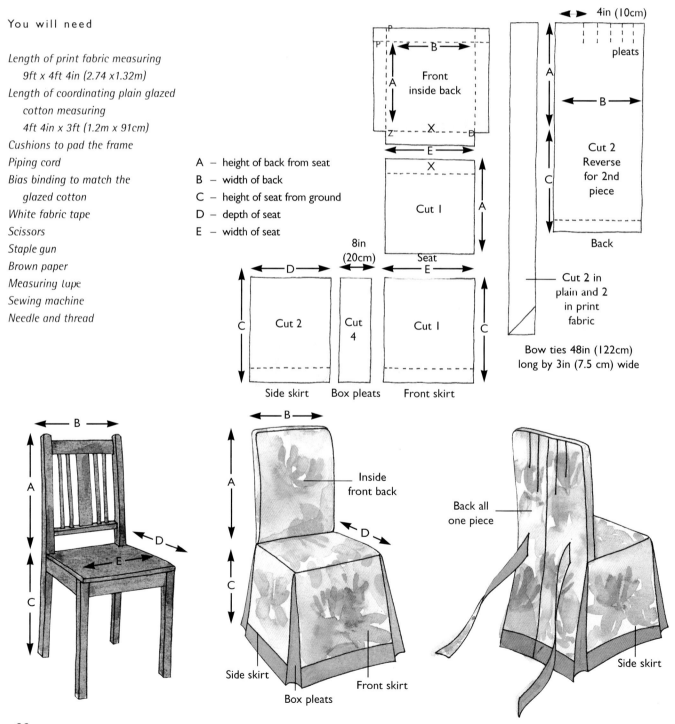

P

Front inside back

A

X

Z   X   D

E

X

Cut 1

A

Seat

8in (20cm)

D

E

C   Cut 2   Cut 4   Cut 1   C

Side skirt   Box pleats   Front skirt

4in (10cm)

pleats

A

B

Cut 2 Reverse for 2nd piece

C

Back

Cut 2 in plain and 2 in print fabric

Bow ties 48in (122cm) long by 3in (7.5 cm) wide

B

A

C

D

E

B

A

Inside front back

D

C

Side skirt   Box pleats   Front skirt

Back all one piece

Side skirt

This kitchen chair had no seat and was destined for the builder's skip when I rescued it. I cut a new piece of plywood to fit the seat and glued and screwed it to the frame. To make the chair more comfortable, I added an old pillow for the back and a cushion for the seat.

1 Measure the back and seat of your chair and find ready made cushions to fit it. Sew pieces of fabric tape to the four corners of the seat cushion and at three points up the side and top edge of the back pillow so the cushions can be tied to the frame. Pull the back cushion tight across the frame and staple along the back side edges.

2 Make a note of the measurements of your chair. Next, following the pattern, cut your fabric to fit adding seam allowances of 1in (2.5cm). Note that the front inside back of the cover is wider than the seat piece by 6in (15cm) to create the box shaped back and it is also

longer by 3in (7.5cm) to take the depth of the seat. Cut matching pieces out of lining. Cut the box pleats out of glazed cotton and lining, two pieces of the bow tie pattern in the flowery fabric and two in the plain fabric.

4 Make up 10ft (3m) of piping using the bias binding.

5 Cut five strips of glazed cotton measuring 3½in (9.5cm) wide the length of the bottom edges for the front, back and side skirt pieces. With right sides facing, seam these to the relevant pieces along the dotted line marked 3in (8cm) from the bottom edges on the cutting pattern.

6 Fold over and press. Lay the front and side skirts, with right sides facing onto their matching lining pieces, and sew a seam around three sides, leaving the top open. Turn the right way out and press.

7 Lay the front inside back piece and seat piece onto its lining

and, with right sides facing, sew together along the lines marked X and Y, and sew Z to Z and 0 to 0 with a 3in (7.5cm) long seam. Cut away the excess fabric on corners and turn the right way out. This piece forms a flap which can be tucked down into the back of the seat between seat cushion pad and the back pillow.

8 On the front inside back piece pin together along the dotted lines bringing P to P and F to F and seam. Cut away any excess fabric. This will form the box shape into which the back pillow will sit.

9 With right sides facing, pin the front and side skirts to the seat piece, sandwiching bias binding between them. Place box pleats on lining pieces with right sides facing and seam along three sides. Turn the right way out and press. Pin the two front box pleats behind the top front and side skirts to span the gap. Tack and seam along the line of

pins securing the box pleats, side skirts and seat piece all in one.

10 With right sides facing, seam the back pieces to their relevant lining pieces along the two long side seams and bottom edge. Turn the right way round and press. Make two pleats in the top of these pieces 4in (10cm) in from the outside edge. Pin and tack pleats in place. Pin one back piece to overlap the other by ½in (1.5cm) and topstitch to secure the position of the pleats, and this overlap, with a seam ½in (1.5cm) in from the top raw edge.

11 With right sides facing and sandwiching the bias binding in between the pieces, tack, pin and then seam together the two back pieces with the front inside back piece. Clip away excess fabric and turn the right way round.

12 With right sides facing, place the bow pieces onto the glazed cotton backing and sew around the two long sides and along the

diagonal short width. Turn the right way out and press. Tuck in the raw edges at the open ends and slipstitch together. Attach these ends to the back of the chair in positions marked Y on the diagram with a hand sewn slipstitch.

13 Turn the cover inside out, pin the two back box pleats in place. Seam to the seat piece on one side and slipstitch to the inside of the back pieces on the other side.

14 Turn the cover the right way out, press and slip over the chair. Tie a beautiful bow to hold the two back pieces together.

Swags and tails cut on the bias

Like so many of the simplest ideas, this is one I hit upon by chance, when I had to convert a circular tablecloth into swags and tails, as the fabric that matched existing curtains had been discontinued. The pelmet hangs in delightful soft rhythmic folds, creating a look that can only be achieved with fabric cut on the bias.

Swag Pattern

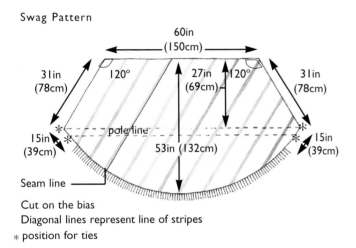

60in (150cm)
31in (78cm)   120°   27in (69cm)   120°   31in (78cm)
pole line
15in (39cm)   53in (132cm)   15in (39cm)
Seam line
Cut on the bias
Diagonal lines represent line of stripes
∗ position for ties

Tail Pattern   This is cut out of a perfect quarter circle using the full 48in (120cm) width

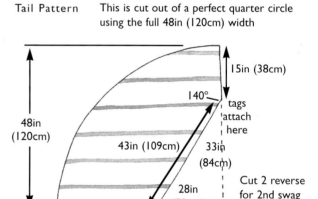

15in (38cm)
140°   tags attach here
48in (120cm)   43in (109cm)   33in (84cm)
28in (72cm)   Cut 2 reverse for 2nd swag

Fringe is sewn along curve and across bottom 27in (68cm) measurement

You will need

Curtain pole to fit your window
Curtain fabric and silk lining to fit your window
Fringing
Sewing machine
Brown paper
White fabric tape
Scissors
Pencil
Sewing machine
Needle and thread

Unlike traditional pelmets, which have to be fixed in place with Velcro or staples, this pelmet is easy to make, arrange and remove for cleaning.

1 Make a template from brown paper, following the pattern for one swag and one tail. As you will need to join pieces of fabric to make the swag, cut the pattern out of two pieces of brown paper, dividing the pattern along the seam line, and adding a ½in (1.5cm) seam allowance.

2 Cut one swag and two tails out of the main fabric, reversing the pattern for the second tail. Line up the arrows on the diagrams with the straight grain of the fabric. Repeat with the silk lining fabric.

3 With right sides facing, seam the swag pieces together, repeat for the silk lining. Lay the lining pieces on the main fabric, with right sides facing, and sew a ½in (1.5cm) seam around all edges, leaving a gap for turning.

4 Clip the seam along the curves and cut off the pointed ends of the tails. Turn the pieces the right way out, press the seams and slipstitch the gaps.

5 Pin and tack the fringing to the front edges of the tails and the bottom edge of the swag. Slipstitch the fringe firmly in place following the fringe line drawn on the pattern.

6 Cut the fabric tape into eight lengths measuring 9in (23cm) and sew two lengths to the top of each tail and four lengths to the swag as shown on the pattern. Tie in place on the pole.

7 Hang your curtains on the track behind the pelmet.

Distressed wall cabinet

Painted period furniture is much sought by collectors and increasingly expensive to buy. This is an ingeniously easy way of artificially ageing new woodwork with paint to give a modern piece antique character and charm.

You will need

Pine or Medium Density Fibre board (MDF) wall cabinet
Terracotta emulsion paint
Blue-grey emulsion paint
Acrylic varnish
Acrylic convertor
Sandpaper
White candle
Medium paintbrush
Natural sponge
Saucers

The colours you choose are extremely important – this combination of blue-grey paint on a terracotta base is particularly successful.

1 Sand the shelving unit to get rid of any rough edges. Make absolutely sure that the cupboard doors open and close easily, as an extra coat of paint will increase any jamming problem.

2 Apply a coat of the terracotta paint to the exterior surfaces and leave to dry.

3 Rub the terracotta paint in patches with the candle, paying attention to those areas that would over the course of years have received the most wear and tear, in particular around the handles and along the mouldings and side edges.

4 Next apply a second coat of the blue-grey emulsion, and you will notice that the paint will not adhere to the waxed surfaces, allowing the terracotta paint to show through.

5 When the second coat has dried, use the sandpaper to soften any areas where the second coat looks too solid or the line between colours is too severe.

6 Use the blue-grey emulsion to paint the inside and doors of the cupboard and sponge the china door knobs.

7 When this has dried, apply a protective coating of acrylic varnish to all surfaces.

8 Apply a coat of acrylic convertor to the door knobs following the directions on the tin. Sponge with blue-grey emulsion and protect with a coat of acrylic varnish.

Decoupage tray

For evening drinks on a special occasion, this decoupage tray, decorated with eighteenth century print room designs and protected by several coats of varnish, is elegantly stylish and deceptively hardwearing.

You will need

Tray
Motif cutouts
Sandpaper
Primer
Black eggshell oil based paint
PVA glue
Shellac
Oil based ageing varnish
Crackle varnish
Acrylic varnish
Paintbrush
Bowl of warm water
Tea bag
Dry clean cloth

Decoupage is a method of decorating objects with paper cutouts overlaid with many coats of varnish. To achieve an inlaid ivory on ebony effect, restrict your choice of cutouts to black and white designs. If you do resort to photocopies, which can work wonderfully, insist on top quality paper as inferior papers will buckle. The true art of decoupage lies in the patient application of varnish — as many as twenty coats for the best results — and very precise scissor work.

1 Rub down the tray with sandpaper and apply a coat of primer.

2 When this has dried paint the tray with a coat of the black eggshell paint and leave to dry. Seal the tray with shellac varnish to prevent paint from staining the paper cutouts.

3 Cut out the motifs and position your design. Make a rough tracing to record the position of each cutout. Mitre the border corners and number the backs of the border pieces to remind you of the order in which to stick them down.

4 When you are happy with the design, dip each piece in warm water for a few seconds. If you wish the paper to appear aged, add a soggy tea bag to the water.

5 Taking one piece of paper at a time, dab off the excess water with a cloth, apply PVA glue to the back and stick the paper in the correct position. Clean up any excess glue around the edges. When you have completed the design, leave the tray to dry overnight.

6 Apply at least five or six coats of shellac to seal and protect the paper cutouts.

7 If you wish to create an antiqued look, apply a thin coat of ageing varnish and allow to dry. Finish off with a crackle glaze (*see page 140*).

Easy café curtains and wooden pelmet

Dressing a small window to make it look interesting is always a challenge. This shaped wooden pelmet and tab headed café curtain is one way to create a fresh country look.

You will need

Decorative pelmet board to fit the width of your window
Plywood measuring 6in (15cm) wide to fit the length of your window
Two shelf brackets measuring 4in (10cm)
Woodworking glue
Jigsaw
Panel pins
Screws
Cream vinyl emulsion paint
Artist's acrylic paint in permanent green
Fabric cut to the same width as your curtain and measuring 10in (26cm) deep
Staple gun
Artist's paint brush
Brown paper
Scissors
Pencil
Striped fabric measuring 3ft (1m)
Twelve eyelets
Iron-on tape
Iron and ironing board
Wooden dowelling
Two brass cupboard rail sockets
Dressmaker's pins
Sewing machine
Needle and thread

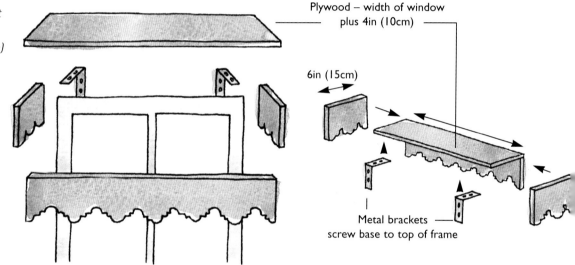

Plywood – width of window plus 4in (10cm)

6in (15cm)

Metal brackets screw base to top of frame

WOODEN PELMET

1 Cut the decorative board to fit the width of the window, adding 4in (10cm) to clear the window recess.

2 Cut two pieces of plywood to the same depth as the decorative board and measuring 6in (5cm) wide, making sure to include the thickness of the decorative board.

3 Screw the shelf brackets to the outer edges of the top piece of plywood and glue and panel pin the four pieces together to make the box shaped pelmet.

4 Paint the pelmet and allow to dry. Then draw around the decorative edge of the pelmet onto the piece of brown paper and cut out carefully. Place the template above the bottom edge of the pelmet allowing an even border of 2in (5cm).

5 Trace the pattern onto the finished pelmet and, using the artist's brush, paint the border using the permanent green acrylic paint.

6 Before screwing the pelmet to the wall, turn in the raw edges of the frill and gather it along the top edge. Staple the frill to the back side of the pelmet and finally, screw the pelmet firmly in position.

CAFÉ CURTAINS

The eyelet tab headings I used for these café curtains are an easy alternative for non-sewers who can use iron-on tape to bind raw edges..

1 Cut the dowelling to fit your window recess. Screw the brass sockets at café curtain height and slot the dowelling in place.

2 Measure the distance from the rod to the sill and add 8in (20cm) for the top and bottom for hem allowance. Using the full width of the fabric, cut a piece to fit the window and turn under a top and bottom hem.

3 Mark the position of the eyelets, using the stripes as markers, by placing pins evenly along the top edge of the curtain. Allow the fabric to create pleats between pins and leave 1in (2.5cm) for side hems. Trim any excess fabric and topstitch the side hems.

4 Tack along the pin lines and topstitch the pleats in place. Insert the eyelets along the top of the curtain.

5 Cut six tabs measuring 1ft x 6in (30 x 15cm). Make a $\frac{1}{2}$in (1cm) turning along the top, bottom and one side edge, tuck in the raw edges and topstitch in place. Fold the tabs lengthways so that the remaining raw edge is covered by the finished edge, topstitch in place.

6 Thread the tabs through the eyelets, over the pole and back through the same eyelet.

Stencilled mirror sconce

It is amazingly easy to transform a plain, flat, circular mirror and cupboard rail socket into this delightful imitation lapis lazuli sconce, stencilled with gold leaf.

You will need

Plain flat mirror
Brass cupboard rail socket
White acrylic paint
Indigo blue artist's acrylic paint
Ultramarine artist's acrylic paint
Gold paint
Acrylic scumble
Fine sandpaper
Stencil brush
Natural sponge
Sheet of acetate
Sheet of bevelled-edge glass
Tracing paper to fit your mirror
    frame
Hot pen
Pencil
Felt tip pen
Gold or metal size
Dutch metal
Acrylic varnish
Masking tape
Old saucers or plastic pots
Ruler

I used a flat round mirror made from Medium Density Fibreboard (MDF). This has no grain and is easier to disguise as stone but any sort of mirror frame which can be painted will do.

1 Paint the mirror frame with two coats of the white paint. Mix equal quantities of the indigo blue acrylic paint with the acrylic scumble in a saucer or pot, and stir in some of the white paint.

2 Apply this mixture to the frame with delicate, controlled sweeping and dabbing motions until it is completely covered.

3 While this is still wet, mix equal quantities of the ultramarine acrylic paint with the acrylic scumble and, using a sponge, apply this with a lightly controlled sweeping motion to create darker, richer areas of colour.

4 When this has dried, spatter the frame with gold paint by knocking a fully loaded stencil brush against a ruler.

5 To make the stencil, trace the pattern below and use a photo-copier to enlarge the pattern to fit your frame size. Lay a second sheet of tracing paper on the frame and trace around it to create an outline. Position the cupboard rail socket in the centre of the traced frame and draw around it in pencil.

6 Lay the photocopied stencil below the traced shape of the frame and, with the felt tip pen, transfer the stencil to fit either side of the cupboard rail socket.

7 Lay the glass over the completed tracing. Place the acetate on top of the glass and secure with masking tape. Trace

the outline of the stencil with the hot iron, cutting the acetate.

8 Position the screw holes for the cupboard rail sockets.

9 Place the stencil over the frame and, using a brush, stipple with the size. Wait until the glue is tacky to touch, then peel a sheet of Dutch metal from its backing, lay it over the size and rub lightly, allowing the excess size to flake away and making sure that the stencilled area is thoroughly covered.

10 Remove the stencil and leave to dry overnight. Finish with two coats of the varnish. Screw the cupboard rail socket in place and heat the bottom of the candle before easing it into the cup-board rail socket.

Three hour thrills

Using simple techniques and readily available materials, here are seven eminently worthwhile projects. The coronet headboard is particularly easy if you can fix a shelf and sew a straight edge, and the Dutch tile table top and Swedish chest both employ a simple paint roller trick, which is breathtakingly effective.

Coronet carved headboard

Old hand carved wooden mouldings offer limitless decorative potential as luxurious headboards from which to suspend bedroom drapes. As an affordable alternative, most good timber merchants stock reproductions of old designs and you can of course stain or distress them for an antique look.

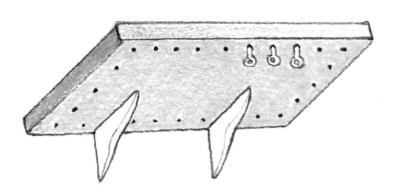

You will need

Twenty six 1in (2.5cm) eyelet hooks

Two metal shelf brackets

Medium Density Fibreboard (MDF) or timber shelf measuring 1in (2.5cm) thick

Decorative wooden carving

Wood glue

Panel pins

Six lengths of curtain fabric measuring 6ft (2m)

Simple gathered curtain heading tape

Scissors

Needle and thread

Sewing machine

To completely transform this country style bedroom, I also lined the walls in a delicate geometric fabric to go with the cottage sprig chintz used to make the bed drapes.

1 Cut your shelf to size, mine was 4½ x 11in (12 x 29cm), and attach the shelf brackets.

2 Screw the eyelet hooks at ½in (1cm) intervals into the underside of the shelf.

3 Next, fix the carving to the front edge with the glue and the panel pins.

4 Turn the shelf the right way up and screw the metal brackets to the wall, centred over the bed and about 5ft 8in (1.8m) above the floor. If the wall is fabric lined, as shown here, you will need to screw special battens between the fabric and wall to hold the screws.

5 Make three simple curtains measuring 5ft 8in (1.8m) long. These will be hidden from view behind the bed so they don't need to be any longer.

6 First make the curtain for the back section from a double fabric width sewn together along one

long edge. Make two turns along the top raw edges to the back of the fabric, and seam the gathering tape along the front top edge of the fabric.

7 Make the two side curtains, using single widths, and line each with another width of the same fabric.

8 Head the curtains with standard gathered curtain tape, fold the top raw edges into the wrong sides and hem along the bottom raw edges. Pull up the curtain tape and attach it to the eyelet hooks with ordinary curtain hooks.

Simple screens

If you need to hide an untidy corner or divide a large living space into separate cosy dining and seating areas , screens can play a useful part in modern interiors.

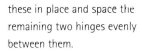

You will need

Three wooden panels measuring
*   1ft 6in x 5ft (52 x 46cm)*
Eight flush mounted hinges and
*   screws*
Bradawl
Screwdriver
Jigsaw
Sandpaper
White vinyl silk emulsion
Acrylic glaze
Artist's acrylic paint in phthalo
*   green and cobalt blue*
Stencil of a tree in a terracotta pot
*   measuring 26 x 16in (66 x 40cm)*
Border stencil measuring
*   6in (5cm) wide*
Stencil paints in Delft blue,
*   mid-green, poppy red,*
*   bright yellow, burnt umber*
*   and titanium white*
Stencil brushes
Masking tape
Acrylic varnish
Pencil
Brown paper
Kitchen roll
Old saucers or plastic pots

If you cannot find a matching set of old or new matching doors, Medium Density Fibreboard (MDF) can be sawn into a simple rectangular shape with a decorative serpentine shaped top edge.

1 Cut brown paper to measure 18 x 12in (46 x 30cm) and fold in two to find the centre. Open out the paper and, using a large plate or edge of a lampshade as a template, draw a curve centred on the fold. Fold again and draw a gentle sloping line to join the end of the curve to the edge of the paper. Use this as a template to cut three identical curves with the jigsaw at the top of each screen panel. Sandpaper any rough edges.

2 Paint both sides of the screen panels with two coats of white vinyl emulsion and leave to dry.

3 Mark positions for the hinges. Start with the top and bottom hinges which are set 4in (10cm) from the outside edges, screw

these in place and space the remaining two hinges evenly between them.

4 Mix one large cupful of glaze with a teaspoon of each of the green and blue acrylic artist's paints. Paint the screen in vertical lines, making sure your brush strokes are even and straight. Leave to dry.

5 Start stencilling the terracotta pot on the front panel. For the pot try using the burnt umber mixed with the poppy red and shading with the mid-green at the edges to create a three dimensional effect. Mix all three colours and add a touch of blue to create the earth colour. Stencil the stem in raw umber with green shading along one edge.

6 For the back of the screen work out exactly where your border design will start and finish; this one is set 6in (15cm) from the top and bottom edge. Secure the first stencil in position with masking tape and apply the stencil paint. Do not worry if the colours overlap slightly, as extra shading will enrich the final result. Be careful to use dry brushes, and always dab the brush onto an old rag or absorbent paper before applying to the screen.

7 Leave the stencil paints to dry and apply two coats of acrylic varnish.

Shelf table

This elegant bracketed shelf table is ideal as a hall telephone table, to flank a double bed or to use beside a sofa to hold drinks and table lamps, particularly in a room with limited living space.

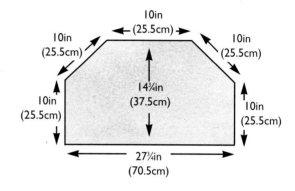

SEMICIRCULAR TABLE

You will need

Semicircular piece of Medium Density Fibreboard (MDF) ¹/₂in (1.5cm) thick
Length of half round moulding to fit table edge
Panel pins or tacks
Tack hammer
Shelf bracket
Screws
Wall plugs
Screwdriver
Electric drill
Off-white emulsion paint
Artist's acrylic paint
Acrylic glaze
Acrylic varnish
Medium paintbrush
Stippling brush
Cotton rags
Old saucer or plastic pot

It is important to make sure you have the right bracket to help you create the look you want for this table. I found a ready made design in MDF but there are plenty of alternatives to be found made in wrought iron, carved wood, or plaster. You can always vary the size of the table top to suit the size of the bracket. The one I used had a diameter of 2ft (60cm) but some timber merchants sell ready made round chipboard or MDF table tops which can easily be cut in two to make a pair of shelf tables.

1 Cut the moulding to the length of the curved edge and bend gently to fit. If you need to make joins in the moulding, try to cut them at a 45° angle and fill the crack with wood filler. Carefully fix the moulding in place with the tacks and the tack hammer. It is important to use this special hammer; otherwise you may split the moulding.

2 Paint the table top and the bracket with one or two coats of off-white emulsion. Leave to dry.

3 Mix half a teaspoon of the artist's acrylic paint with six teaspoons of the acrylic glaze in an old saucer. Paint this mixture over the table top using the household paint brush. While the glaze is still wet, dab the stippling brush over the glaze to give the surface a fine texture and remove any brush marks. As the glaze builds up on the brush, wipe it off with an old rag.

4 Before the glaze dries, twist a clean cotton rag and roll it over the stippled surface, just as you would roll a rolling pin. Dab the cloth along the side of the moulding to produce a similar effect.

5 Repeat the stippling method for the bracket, but do not rag roll it. When the glaze is dry apply two coats of varnish.

6 Screw the bracket to the base of the shelf, drilling the holes first to prevent the MDF from splitting.

7 Prepare the wall, using wall plugs if necessary, before fixing the shelf in place.

CORNERED TABLE

This five sided table with a plaster bracket is a formal alternative to the circular shape, It is fixed to the wall with iron brackets.

Limed and stencilled dressing table

The pretty gothic shape of this oak table called for a feminine approach, so I limed it and designed this border stencil of ribbons, bows and roses for the top. To achieve an antique look, I softened the stencil with sandpaper.

You will need

Liming wax
Copper wire hand brush
Fine steel wool
Sandpaper
Stencil paints and brushes
Acrylic varnish
Sheet of bevelled-edge glass
Tracing paper
Felt tip pen
Pencil
Sheet of acetate
Hot pen
Masking tape
Cloth or kitchen roll

By using three separate stencilled images, like this rose, bow and ribbon, that can be cut out as separate stencils and enlarged or reduced, you can create a border pattern will fit any size or shape of table.

1 Cut a piece of tracing paper to the exact size of your table. On a separate sheet of tracing paper, use a felt tip pen to copy your chosen motifs and, using a photocopier, enlarge them to the size you need.

2 Cut the stencils out of acetate, using the hot pen and glass (*see page 72*).

3 Transfer these onto the tracing paper cut to the size of your table top, using a pencil while you plot your design and then finishing with a felt tip pen. You can cut a master stencil out of acetate, or decide to use your master tracing for this purpose.

4 Make sure the table top is clean and free of any old paint or varnish. Work the copper brush along the direction of the wood to open the grain and remove the soft pulp.

5 Dip the steel wool into the liming wax and, rubbing in every direction, apply it to the table. Leave to dry for ten minutes and then remove any excess wax with a fresh piece of steel wool, leaving wax in the grooves of the grain, but cleaning the surface. Protect with a coat of acrylic varnish.

6 Lay your master stencil over the table top and use it as a guide to position and secure the separate ribbon, bow and rose stencils with masking tape.

7 Stencil the images using a different brush for each colour. The brushes must be very dry, so dab the brush onto a piece of cloth or kitchen towel before applying the paint and set the first dab of the brush into the centre of an image away from the edges. Do not worry if the colours overlap as this produces delicate shading and adds to the final antiqued effect.

8 When the paint is dry, rub the images with sandpaper to create a worn look. Finally, apply a coat of acrylic varnish.

Dutch tile table top

Small garden tables always come in handy. You can find junk tables with uneven or damaged tops quite easily, but make sure the one you choose is structurally sound with a pretty base. Here is a way to redeem a table base by giving it a Dutch tile top.

You will need

Second hand table
Medium Density Fibreboard (MDF) top
Half round timber moulding ½in (1.5cm) thick
Hammer
Wood glue
Panel pins
Screwdriver
Screws
Bradawl
Four MDF decorative brackets
Resin filler
White matte emulsion paint
Yellow ochre matte emulsion paint
Khaki matte emulsion paint
Emerald green stencil paint
Pale mint green emulsion paint
Royal blue stencil paint
Tile stencil measuring 6 x 6in (15 x 15cm)
Stencil brush
Masking tape
Medium paintbrush
Small paint roller and tray
Ruler or tape measure
Acrylic varnish
Outdoor varnish

As I needed my tiles to be 6 x 6in (15 x 15cm), I cut the MDF board to 27 x 20in (59 x 51cm) which allowed for a pretend grouting of ½in (1.5cm). To hide the existing top the new top should be bigger by at least 4in (10cm) all the way round.

1 Cut the half round moulding into four pieces, and mitre the ends to fit the corners of the new table top. Glue and panel pin the moulding in place and screw the new top on to the old one.

2 To strengthen the base, stick the four decorative brackets to the inside top of the legs, butting them on to the under-side of the table frame. Fill the joins with a resin filler.

3 Paint the table base with a couple of coats of the khaki paint and leave to dry. Using a stencil brush, stipple the darker emerald green over the base. Next, stipple the pale mint green to fill in the gaps, and overlap the darker tone of green to create an oxidized copper effect.

4 Paint the table top with a couple of coats of the white emulsion. Using a ruler and pencil divide the table top into twelve tiles, leaving a border of ½in (1.5cm) around each tile and a 2in (5cm) border around the four sides of the table. Mask these pretend grouting lines with masking tape.

5 Paint the table top in one coat of the yellow ochre emul-sion, taking care to leave no traces of white, and leave to dry.

6 To create the hand fired tile effect, load the paint roller with the white emulsion, and apply a patchy light coating over the table top allowing some of the yellow ochre colour to show through. Leave to dry.

7 Remove the masking tape and position the tile stencil between the grouting lines taping it firm-ly in place. Stencil a Dutch flower tile design in the blue paint. Repeat for each tile and leave to dry.

8 Finally, apply two coats of protective varnish. If you intend the table to be for outdoor use, make sure to apply a final coat-ing of waterproof floor varnish, but remember not to leave the table outside in frosty weather.

Fabric wallhanging

Old tapestries, Chinese embroideries and early American quilts make beautiful wall hangings, but cost a lot, whereas a moden fabric in a rich intricate design framed in a mount looks striking and adds a luxurious feel to any room.

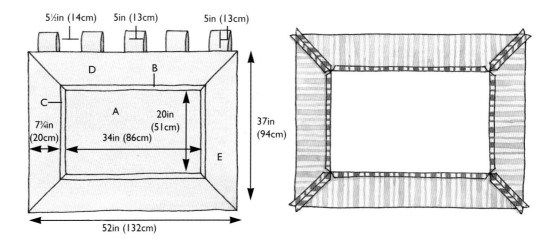

You will need

Length of patterned fabric measuring 2ft (61cm)
Length of plain fabric in a coordinating colour measuring 10in (26cm)
Length of striped fabric measuring 6ft (83cm)
Interlining measuring 3ft 2in x 4ft 5in (1 x 1.3m)
Black metal curtain pole
Scissors
Sewing machine
Needle and thread

1 Following the pattern but adding a seam allowance of ½in (1.5cm) all round, cut one centre piece out of the patterned fabric. Cut two strips, B and C, from the plain edging and cut two pieces, D and E, out of the striped fabric. Cut a piece of the striped fabric and the interlining for the backing piece.

2 Mitre pieces D and E to form a complete square and mitre pieces B and C. Leave a ½in (1.5cm) gap at the inside end of each seam. Press open the mitred seams and turn under all the raw edge, using up the full seam allowance and press. Turn under the raw edges of the main piece in the same way and press.

3 Lay the backing piece with the wrong side facing the interlining.

Next lay the striped wide framed piece onto the backing piece, with right sides facing, and seam along three sides leaving the top long seam open. Turn the right way out and press.

4 Lay the remaining pieces onto the backing piece, and pin, tack and topstitch the pieces in position, leaving the top edge open.

5 To make the tabs cut five pieces measuring 11 x 11in (28 x 28cm) out of the striped fabric. With right sides facing, fold in half lengthways, sew a ½in (1.5cm) seam along the long edges turn, turn the right way out. Fold each tab in two and tuck ½in (1.5cm) of the raw ends into the gap between the two layers of fabric at the top edge, positioning them at equal spaces

5½in (14cm) apart. The two tabs should sit 3in (8cm) in from the outside edges and all stripes on

the tabs should be carefully matched up with stripes on the main fabric.

6 Topstitch the tabs firmly in place, sewing as close to the top edge as possible.

7 Press the completed wall hanging and slide it onto the curtain pole.

Swedish chest

Of all of the decorative country styles, Swedish Gustavian is one of the most enduring and there is nothing more satisfying than painting plain furniture to create the piece you wanted and perhaps could not afford. This simple plywood chest was transformed with Scandinavian colours, a simple framed front panel and a fruit swag stencil.

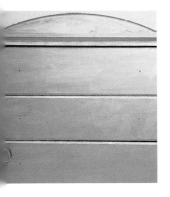  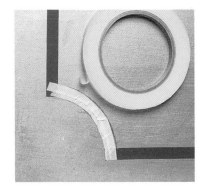 

You will need

Gold paint
Off-white emulsion paint
Gustavian green emulsion paint
Masking tape
Flexicurve
Pencil
Ruler
Acrylic varnish
Fruit swag stencil
Small paint roller and tray
Wire wool
Dark-blue stencil paint
Cadmium yellow pigment
Stencil brushes
Crackle varnish
Gilt cream or artist's acrylic paint in raw umber
Old rag or kitchen roll
Old saucers or plastic pots

1 Remove the drawer knobs and paint the entire surface of the chest and drawer fronts with two coats of the gold paint.

2 Use a ruler and tape to mask out a gold line and create a large panel in the centre of the drawer front. The top line of tape is set 3½in (9cm) in from the top of the first drawer and bottom of the last drawer, and stops 4in (10cm) short of the sides of the chest.

3 Use the flexicurve and a pencil to make the crescent shapes at the top two corners of the panel. Bend the curve to join the ends of the straight tape and pencil parallel curved lines using the thickness of the flexicurve.

4 Cut the masking tape in half lengthways and press the uncut edge against the pencil lines to mask the curved corners.

5 Paint the centre panel with a coat of the off-white emulsion, applying the paint sparingly with the small roller to create a patchy effect allowing the gold to show through.

6 Using the paint roller and tray in the same way as Step 5, apply the green emulsion paint over the remaining surfaces outside the edges of the panel.

7 When the paint has dried, rub the wire wool across the middle of each drawer to create a worn wood grained effect.

8 Stencil the drawer fronts. Secure the stencil with masking tape and, using the roller still loaded with the green emulsion paint, roll over the entire stencil. The roller must be damp, not wet, so take off any excess wash on a piece of kitchen roll or an old rag before stencilling.

9 Add the detail to the stencil, stippling the green for leaves, blue for bows, off-white for the flower heads and yellow pigment to pick out highlights in the oranges. Do not worry if colours overlap as this adds to the mellowed antique effect.

10 Remove all tape, and paint the chest with crackle varnish (*see page 139*). When this is dry rub gilt cream or raw umber into the cracks. Finally, paint the knobs with the green emulsion paint and rub with the gilt cream.

Evening escapades

Irrespective of your energy levels, evening projects should by definition help you unwind after a busy day. Here are four to choose from; each is appropriately undemanding and absorbing. Cutting the mosaic stencil with a hot pen is particularly soothing and applying gold leaf is most satisfying. If you enjoy sewing, the dining chair cover yields good returns in being dashingly effective and dazzlingly easy.

Quick and easy dining chair cover

Just one yard or metre of luxury fabric and two silk ties can transform a metal folding chair into a decorative dining chair. Considering how easily they can be packed away or hung on the wall when not in use, these chairs are a terrific plus.

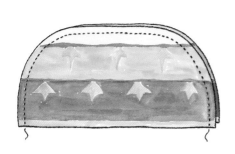

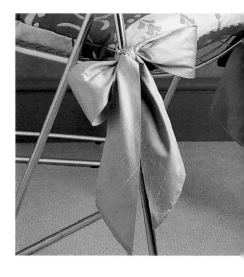

You will need

Length of fabric measuring 3ft
Two lengths of plain silk measuring
*   2ft (60cm) in contrasting colours*
Cushion pad to fit the size of
your chair seat
Sewing machine
Saucer
Brown paper
Felt tip pen
Scissors
Tailor's chalk
Needle and thread

1 Make a paper template by placing the brown paper against the chair back and drawing around it with a black felt tip pen. Add a 1/2in (1.5cm) seam allowance all round and cut out the paper pattern.

2 Cut two pieces of the fabric to size and, with right sides facing, tack around the curved edge.

3 Place the shape on the chair and adjust to fit. Machine and then clip the seam allowance, turn the right way out and press. Hem the raw edges and press.

4 To make the cushion seat fold a piece of fabric in half with right sides facing. Then trace around the cushion, adding a seam allowance of 1/2in (1.5cm). Use a saucer to round off the two front corners, and cut out two pieces of fabric.

5 For the ties cut eight strips of silk measuring 24 x 41/2 in (61 x 12cm). Cut one end of each strip at a 45° angle.

6 Take two of the strips and, with right sides facing, sew together along the long sides and diagonal ends, taking a 1/2in (1cm) seam allowance. Clip away the excess fabric at the pointed ends, turn the right way out and press. Repeat for the remaining six strips, making four ties in all.

7 Place the front and back cushions pieces together with right sides facing. Position the

gathered ends of two ties in between the cushion pieces, 1/2in (l.5cm) in from the straight raw back edge.

8 Pin the cushion pieces together, tack and then sew around all four sides, taking a 1/2in (1.5cm) seam allowance and sew through the raw ends of all four ties. Turn the right way out and press.

9 Slip the cushion pad into the cover, turn in the edges of the opening and slipstitch to close.

Mosaic table top

Mosaic tables are notoriously expensive, so here is an affordable trompe l'oeil alternative that makes an ideal conservatory table top for summer drinks.

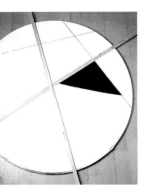    

You will need

Round table top

Length of reeded moulding measuring 8ft 6in x ½ in (2.6m x 1.5cm)

Panel pins

Tack hammer

Vinyl silk white emulsion paint

Black emulsion paint

Acetate sheets

Sheet of bevelled-edge glass

Hot pen or small craft knife

Large metal ruler

Three pieces of tracing paper

Felt tip pen

Pencil

Stencil paints in aquamarine and marine blue

Small paint roller and tray

Damp cloth

Old rag or absorbent paper

Clear gloss varnish

I used a plain chipboard table top with a diameter of 2ft 7in (79cm) teamed it with an old metal base, and painted it in shades of cool blues. The mosaic pattern is created with a two layer stencil. You can buy ready made stencil mosaics, but as no two pieces of tile are ever exactly the same, the drawing and cutting lines should be deliberately uneven. Therefore it is well worth attempting to design and cut the stencil yourself.

1 Paint the table top with two coats of the white emulsion and paint the reeded moulding with the black emulsion.

2 Wrap the reeded moulding around the diameter of the table top to cover the raw edge and fix it with panel pins. Cut any joins at a 45° angle, hide the gaps between the joins with wood filler and touch up with the black paint.

3 Find the centre of the table by drawing two straight lines to cross each other along the outside edges of the circle. Draw two lines through the centre point of each line at a right angle. The point where these lines cross is the centre of the table. Cut a piece of tracing paper to fit into a quarter segment of the table, and draw out your design with the felt tip pin. Work out which shapes to cut out of the first stencil and which to cut out of the second stencil, separating the two colours. Number these pieces accordingly and mark the centre of the table with an X.

4 Lay the tracing paper under the glass, place the acetate on top and secure with masking tape. Draw round the shapes for the first stencil with the hot pen and mark the centre of the table on the stencil with the felt tip.

5 Cut out the second stencil in exactly the same way, again marking the centre of the table.

6 Place the first stencil on the table, lining up the centre marks carefully, and secure with masking tape. Load the paint roller, roll it over an old rag until there is hardly any paint left on the roller, and paint over the stencil. Before the paint dries, remove some of the paint by wrapping your finger in the damp cloth and working through the stencil to create a patchy effect that is characteristic of real mosaic. Lift off the stencil carefully.

7 Repeat this process in the other paint colour for the second stencil. If you find any paint has seeped under the stencils, take a fine paint brush, dip it in the white emulsion and paint over any blotches.

8 Cover the table top with at least two coats of the gloss varnish and screw the table on to its base.

Floor standing candlesticks

Turning an item destined for the skip into something worth keeping is an exciting challenge. Balusters left over from renovating a staircase or old table and chair legs can make sensational floor standing candlesticks.

You will need

Baluster or old chair or table leg
Three timber squares measuring
3 x 3in (8 x 8cm), 4¼ x 4¼in
(11 x 11 cm) and 6 x 6in
(15 x 15cm)
Metal night light holder
Small hand saw
Electric drill
Flat 1½in (3.5cm) drill bit
Wood glue
Black or terracotta emulsion paint
Small paintbrush
Dutch metal
Flat square brush
Gold size
Fine steel wool
White spirit
Acrylic varnish
Soft stencil brush or cotton wool

I think that these candlesticks look best set side by side in a pair. For maximum visual impact cut them to different heights.

1 Cut the baluster at a point where the design breaks naturally and where it is wide enough for you to drill a 1½in (4cm) hole to hold a chunky candle. For a floor standing candlestick, aim for an overall height of about 2ft 3in (69cm).

2 Make a tiered base out of the timber squares, starting with the biggest and working up to the smallest, gluing them on top of one another, and glue or screw the square base of the baluster to the top of the smallest square. Leave to dry and make sure it is firm.

3 Drill a hole in the top end of the baluster and line with a metal night light holder.

4 Paint the baluster with a coat of paint and leave to dry.

5 Next, paint the baluster with a thin flat brush, applying a thin even layer of gold size, and leave for a few minutes to dry until it feels tacky, rather like the sticky side of adhesive tape. Gold size is white in colour but looks pale blue when applied, and eventually dries to a clear finish.

6 Lay a page of the Dutch metal gently over the size, and rub down carefully with a soft stencil brush or cotton wool. Work out from the middle to remove any air bubbles as you peel away the transfer backing. Don't worry if you do not manage to cover all the paint work, particularly the grooves of the baluster, as you can cover up the bare patches afterwards before the size dries completely. The distressed finish of these candlesticks allows for a few imperfections that will add character to the final result.

7 Dip the fine steel wool in some white spirit and rub in patches over the gilded surface, lifting off some of the gilding and allowing the base colour to show through.

8 Apply three protective coats of acrylic varnish and fit the candle in place.

Stencilled picture frame

Buying and framing pictures can prove to be expensive, yet it is not difficult to give an old picture frame a simple decorative finish. Prints and postcards, framed and hung in clusters and blocks, can make a big impact.

You will need

Flat untreated pine frame
Postcard or print
Blue-grey wood dye
Small paintbrush
Soft cotton cloth
Liming wax
Gilt cream
Steel wool
*Narrow border stencil in a
   classic style*
Stencil brush
Acrylic varnish
Masking tape

I framed this postcard of one of my favourite paintings by Boticelli using a frame that measured 13 x 9in (33 x 23cm) and an eighteenth century Adam design for my border stencil. If you haven't got an old wooden frame at hand, try using a ready made Medium Density Fibreboard (MDF) frame.

1 Paint the frame with one coat of the wood dye and wipe with a cloth to ensure an even distribution of the dye and to reveal the texture of the wood grain underneath. Leave it to dry for twenty minutes.

2 Using the steel wool rub the liming wax onto the frame to produce a cloudy blue-grey effect. Take extra care not to obscure the grain and leave to dry for a further twenty minutes.

3 Taking a clean piece of the soft cloth, carefully rub the gilt cream over the raised, moulded flat edges of the frame.

4 Secure the stencil to the frame with the masking tape and, using the stencil brush, apply the gilt cream sparingly, dabbing off any excess cream onto the soft cloth first.

5 Finally, coat the frame with a protective coat of varnish.

6 Trim your postcard or picture to fit the frame, position it between the glass and backing, and fix it firmly in place.

Weekend wonders

Like everything in life, the more you put in the more spectacular the rewards; so too with the projects in this chapter. None require great skill, but sharing the work with a friend is recommended.

Inlaid marble table

If you love the idea of a marble table, but don't want to spend a fortune, this imitation marble paint effect is the ideal way to give a new lease of life to an old dining table.

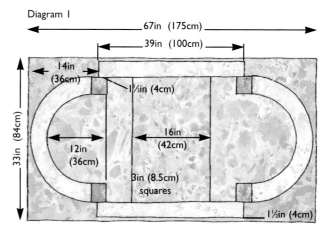

Diagram 1

67in (175cm)
39in (100cm)
14in (36cm)
1½in (4cm)
33in (84cm)
16in (42cm)
12in (36cm)
3in (8.5cm) squares
1½in (4cm)

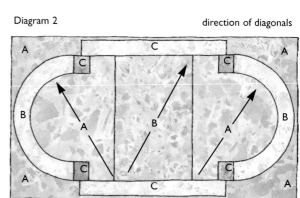

Diagram 2
direction of diagonals

A   C   A
C
B   A   B   A   B
C   C
A   C   A

A - Day 1
B - Day 2 (12 hours later)
C - Day 3 (12 hours later)

INLAY PATTERN

You will need

Off-white oil based eggshell paint
Piece of heavy card or ½in (1cm)
    timber measuring 3in x 3ft 2in
    (8.5 x 98cm)
Small saw
Woodworker's veneer pins
    or panel pins
Metal ruler
Craft knife
Pencil
Masking tape
Strip of narrow moulding
    measuring 1in x 1ft 9in
    (2.5 x 54cm)
White spirit
Clean cloth

If you have a wooden table top you will need to sand it down and then paint it with several coats of oil based off-white eggshell paint, rubbing it down between coats. It may be easier to start afresh with a piece of ¾in (2cm) thick Medium Density Fibreboard (MDF) cut in a rectangular shape measuring 33 x 67in (84cm x 1.7m). Use the panel pins to edge the board with half round ½in (1.5cm) timber moulding and apply a coat of all-purpose primer and two coats of the off-white oil based eggshell, sanding between coats. Finally, screw the table top, from underneath, to the existing base to create a horizontal surface on which to work.

1 Copy the different sections of Diagram 1 onto your table. Use a pencil and card or timber as a template to mark the side borders set 1¹/₂in (4cm) in from the side edges. The borders should be 3ft 2¹/₂in x 3in (98 x 8.5cm).

2 Next, make the compass by nailing a veneer or panel pin into the moulding strip and saw two tiny notches, 3in (8.5cm) apart, at 8¹/₂in (22cm) 11¹/₂in (30.5cm) along the length of the moulding. Nail a veneer pin into the compass point on Diagram 1. Hold the pencil inside the notch furthest from the pin, then swing the strip like a compass to mark the outer circle. Repeat with the pencil in the notch nearest the pin to mark the inner circle line. Finally, use a ruler and pencil to mark the square corner inlays 3 x 3in (8.5 x 8.5cm).

3 When you have finished marking out the design, mask inside the pencilled shapes, including the square inlays, with masking tape. For precise corners, stick masking tape beyond the corners and trim using a scalpel and a metal ruler. To fit the masking tape around the curves, tear off a long strip of tape and stick it to the end of the table. Cut the tape lengthways in two with the scalpel. Pull and bend the tape around the curves butting the uncut machine edge onto the pencil line.

4 Continue until you have masked all the lines as shown. If you make a mistake when drawing the pattern, simply remove the pencil marks with white spirit and a cloth. Do not use a rubber as this will disintegrates into tiny flecks that can get into the glaze.

GLAZES

You will need

Oil glaze
White spirit
Artist's oil colours in emerald green, yellow ochre, raw umber, raw sienna and Venetian red
Four plastic pots
Small paint roller and tray
Large paint roller and tray
Small paintbrush
Newspaper
Artist's fan brush
Artist's pencil brush
Watercolour brush
Softening brush
Rough sandpaper
Mutton cloth or loose weave cotton fabric
Misting spray bottle with adjustable nozzle
Satincoat varnish
Fine steel wool
Hairdryer

1 Stir the oil glaze well, following the instructions on the tin. Next, make the green glaze by squeezing ½in (1cm) of green paint from the tube and mixing it with half a tea cup of glaze. For an authentic look, the grain of the separate blocks of marble should run in different diagonal directions as marked with arrows on Diagram 2.

2 Apply the green glaze with the roller, creating an even ground to one of the large sections marked A on Diagram 1. Next, squeeze a bit of emerald green and raw umber artist's paint into the paint tray, pick up a bit of both colours on the roller and go over the section in the direction of the arrow on Diagram 1.

3 Using the small paintbrush and a mixture of both colours, paint wavy lines more or less in the same diagonal direction.

4 Fold a sheet of newspaper into a fan shape, gently lay it over the wet paint and roll over it firmly with a clean paint roller. Then soften the effect with the softening brush.

5 To create veins in the marble paint effect, first dip the fan brush in the green glaze and then dip it in the splodge of green paint on the roller tray. Using the edge of the brush, draw a broken diagonal line and then twist it as you work to create a wider line using the full width of the brush. Repeat this process with the raw umber paint and soften the effect with the softening brush. To create the paler, almost white veins, which are characteristic of many marbles, wipe the paint off with the clean pencil brush by pushing the brush away from you on the marble effect, twisting it in the same diagonal direction as the other veining.

6 You can also achieve these paler veins with a thumbnail piece of sandpaper, cut into a square measuring ½ x ½in (1 x 1cm), using the guillotine edge with the abrasive side up and opening it out as you did with the fan brush in Step 4.

7 Fill the misting spray bottle with white spirit and squirt this over the painted area while the glaze is still wet. This will form translucent craters; you should soften these immediately with

the brush to stop the spirit from spreading too far.

8 Carefully remove the masking tape around the area you have marbled as soon as you have finished. To avoid damaging the paint under the tape, use the hairdryer to gently warm the tape just before lifting. Carefully wipe off any excess paint. Repeat the marbling process over all sections marked A on Diagram 2 and leave to dry overnight.

9 When all the panels are dry, mask off the panel marked B on Diagram 2. Place masking tape a minuscule distance in from the pencil lines so that a tiny sliver of the previously painted panel shows. This will create an overlap which will look like authentic grouting between real marble blocks. Repeat the marbling process as before, but working on the opposite diagonal. Remove the masking tape while the paint is still wet and wipe off any excess paint.

10 Cover one of the square inlays with the clear glaze using the small paintbrush. Next, dab the emerald green, yellow ochre and raw umber paint straight from the tube onto the square.

Stipple the colours with the small paintbrush to break them up. Next tear off a 4in (10cm) strip of sandpaper and, pressing heavily, wriggle the straight edge over the squares to create a zigzag effect. This produces the malachite inlay effect. Lightly use the softening brush to obliterate any ridges of paint and then remove tape and clean up any excess paint as before. Repeat with the other three square inlays and leave the table to dry overnight.

11 To marble the borders, mask off the outside edges as before. Mix three separate glazes using a quarter of an egg cup of glaze with a blob of artist's oil colour in Venetian red, raw umber and raw sienna. Using the household and fan brushes, paint the Venetian red and raw sienna glazes in alternate stripes over

the border section. With the watercolour brush, dab a little of the raw umber glaze here and there. Next, use the small paintbrush to break up the strokes, and soften the effect with the softening brush.

12 Finally, spray with white spirit as before. Carefully remove all the masking tape and clean up any wet paint that has strayed onto the dry panels. Leave the table to dry. To protect the table, apply two coats of the satincoat varnish, leaving the first to dry overnight. Rub this first coat down with fine steel wool and dust it off before you apply the second coat.

13 Always take care when working with oil based paint and dispose of waste paint in a plastic bag filled with sand.

Decoupage screen

Decoupage is one of the simplest and cheapest types of decorative finish. This handsome screen, decorated in eighteenth century print room motifs, makes a very practical and elegantly distinguished room divider.

You will need

Decoupage motifs for the panels, corner motifs and borders
Medium Density Fibreboard (MDF) boards cut to 1ft 6in x 5ft (46 x 1.52m)
Eight flush mounted hinges and screws
Bradawl
Screwdriver
White vinyl silk emulsion
Artist's acrylic paints in yellow ochre, raw umber and black
Natural sponge
Synthetic sponge
Acrylic glaze
Acrylic varnish
Newspapers
PVA glue
Pasting brush
Small sharp scissors
Soft pencil
Ruler
Plastic pots

The most important element of this screen is the 18th century print room borders and motifs. The ones I used are printed in black on Fabriano Ingres paper, an off-white acid free paper from one of the oldest paper mills in Europe, but there is a wide variety of specially designed packs of decoupage motifs to choose from.

1 First make the screen by marking the positions for the hinges. Start with the top and bottom hinges which are set 4in (10cm) from the outside edges, screw these in place and position the remaining two hinges evenly spaced between them.

2 Paint the panels with three coats of the white paint and leave to dry.

3 Mix one dessertspoon of yellow ochre with half a teaspoon of raw umber and four dessertspoons of the acrylic glaze, paint this onto the screen with the small paintbrush and sponge off with a damp sponge.

4 Dilute the black paint with a little water and paint around the screen edges, the water helps the paint infiltrate the MDF, and leave to dry.

5 Cut out the print room pieces with the sharp scissors, lay out your design and number the pieces in order of how you intend to arrange them.

6 Find the centre of each screen and at the top and bottom mark with a soft pencil where the central panels should go.

7 Before gluing the pieces, dip them in cold water and place them face down on a sheet of newspaper, mopping the excess water away with the clean synthetic sponge. Apply an even layer of the PVA glue to the back of each piece with a pasting brush and, working piece by piece, stick the design firmly in place. As you work, wipe each piece with your hand, working from the centre outwards, to remove bubbles. Wetting the paper first enables each piece to shrink as it dries and results in a tighter grip.

8 Next, using the same technique, glue borders around the central panels, the floral outer borders which edge the screen and the corner pieces. Finally, edge the back of the screen with the border.

9 When the work is completed, apply two coats of acrylic varnish.

French armoire

White melamine cupboards sold in flat packs at amazingly low prices offer huge scope for anyone willing to exploit their decorative potential. Here is one of my favourite transformations, created with a few extra trimmings and an easy woodgrain finish.

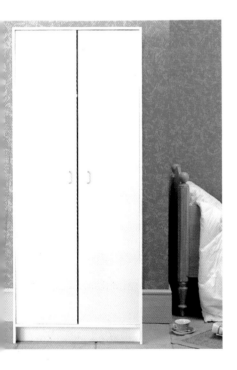  

You will need

Plain two door cupboard
Piece of ¹/₂in (1.5cm) timber
   measuring to fit between the
   bottom shelf and floor around
   the base front, back and two
   sides of the cupboard
Wooden cornice to face the front
   and two sides
Mouldings to panel the two doors
Wooden door knobs
Wood filler
Jigsaw
Panel pins
Wood glue
Hammer

Pine-coloured emulsion paint
Off-white acrylic glaze
Paintbrush
Woodgrainer
Acrylic varnish
Pencil
Card
Scissors
Sandpaper
Screwdriver

You may be lucky enough to find a pair of round or oval frames to fit the width of your cupboard doors. If not use a door moulding kit and then add a cornice, a shaped, scalloped base, new handles and tassels.

1 Cut and mitre the three cornice pieces to fit around the top of the cupboard. Glue and panel pin the cornice in position.

2 Cut the flat timber into three pieces and mitre the corners to fit neatly around the base. Cut the card to half the width of the front bottom edge and, following the pattern shown here, draw and cut out a template. Draw around the template with the pencil on to the wood and cut out the curved shape with a jig-

saw. Sand the edges to a smooth finish and glue and panel pin the shaped base around the bottom of the cupboard.

3 Mark the positions for the panel mouldings on the door fronts, cutting them to fit if necessary, glue them in place and leave to dry. Fill any gaps between the wood joins with wood filler and sand to a smooth finish when dry.

4 Remove the old handles, fill the holes with wood filler, sand to a smooth finish when dry and

screw the new round knob handles in place.

5 Apply two coats of the pine-coloured emulsion paint to all the surfaces of the cupboard and leave to dry.

6 Using the paintbrush apply one coat of the off-white acrylic glaze to one door and, while it is still wet, pull the woodgrainer through the glaze, working down from the top of the door. On every second stripe, pull down and gently rock the woodgrainer half a turn to create a knotted wood effect. Repeat this at odd intervals and occasionally make two plain combed stripes with the graining comb without pivots, and then interject with a stripe of woodgraining. For an authentic wood finish, you need to allow an irregular pattern to form. Apply a coat of glaze to the second door and repeat the woodgrain effect.

7 Apply the off-white glaze to the top cornice and base of the cupboard and run the woodgrainer horizontally following Step 6. As the glaze will take at least twenty minutes to dry, any mistakes can be put right immediately simply by wiping off the glaze with a damp cloth and starting again.

8 When you are happy with your woodgrain effect, leave to dry and finally, seal with a coat of protective varnish.

Stencilled floor and door mat

If you live in a house with old floorboards, the opportunity to experiment with floor designs is worth exploring. Here is a simple floor design to start with, using a border design created with masking tape and a criss-cross stencil of leaves and stars, and just two different shades of wood dye and a trompe l'oeil doormat effect.

STENCILLED FLOOR

You will need

Stencil card and craft knife or bevelled-edged glass, acetate and hot pen
Wood dye in mahogany and dark-oak
Tracing paper
Metal ruler
Spray mount
T-square
String
Drawing pins
Steel tape measure
Pencil
Stencil brushes
Paper towels

Before you begin it is important to remove old stains, varnish and polish from old floorboards by hiring a floor sander. If the boards are beyond saving, then you can lay plywood tiles, or large pieces of chipboard and screw them onto the old floor. Do bear in mind the possibility that the doors will have to be cut down to clear the extra thickness. Once stencilled, the finished floor will need at least four coats of a heavy duty floor varnish to preserve the results of your hard work.

1 Once your floor is sanded and clean, trace and enlarge the stencil designs from this page and make your stencils. You can do

this by transferring the design onto manila paper and cutting them out with a craft knife, or cutting them out of acetate with a hot pen (*see page 72*).

2 Find the centre of the room using two pieces of string. Run them diagonally, from opposite corners, across the room, secure the ends with drawing pins and mark the centre point where they cross with a pencil.

3 Starting from the centre, mark the position for the first stencil star shape and, using the T-square to check angles and the pencil to mark positions, work out a complete design to fit the size of your room. The pattern in

this room runs diagonally across the floorboards but you may find it easier to align the pattern with the direction of your boards.

4 Mark out the border with masking tape. This border is designed to span the width of a 6in (15cm) floorboard but you can alter it to fit your pattern. Use the wider of the two masking tapes to mask the two horizontal lines which edge the border and use the thinner tape for the diagonals. To make sure each triangle is the same, cut a triangle template out of the card to use as a guide. Lay three rows of the thin tape, positioned side by side, to mark the diagonal lines and peeling off the middle tape just before applying the dye. This ensures that the diagonal lines run parallel.

5 Apply spray mount to the back of the leaf and star stencils and, placing the star on the centre mark, begin stencilling. Load your brush lightly and wipe off any excess wood dye onto a paper towel before pouncing the

colour onto the stencil. Use the deep mahogany colour for the central star, stems and base of the leaves. For the tips of the leaves use the dark-oak colour and allow the two colours to overlap and merge, creating a rich dappled effect.

6 When these are dry apply the dark-oak colour to the second layer stencil of the star, producing a shaded three dimensional effect.

7 Following your pencil lines repeat this process, using the T-square to double check all right angles until the entire floor is stencilled.

8 Use the same shade of wood dyes to stencil the border, mahogany for the triangles and dark-oak for the diagonal lines. To finish off the border design, use the star motif in the corners of the room, framing it in a square created with the thicker masking tape. When the border is complete, peel away all the masking tape, and apply three coats of heavy duty varnish. Leave to dry between coats following the directions on the tin.

STENCILLED DOORMAT

You will need

Wood dye in deep-blue, red, green,
  yellow, charcoal, bronze and jade
Stencil brushes
Stencil card and craft knife
  or bevelled-edged glass, acetate
  and hot pen
Tracing paper
Spray mount
Soft pencil
Metal ruler
Paper towels
Two rolls of masking tape in
  different widths
Floor varnish

A trompe l'oeil rug placed in a hall is a lot easier to keep looking clean than the real thing, providing it is layered with coats of heavy duty floor varnish. If you want to save time, you can buy ready made stencils but old rugs and kelims are a wonderful source of inspiration if you fancy trying to create your own look.

1 Photocopy and enlarge the stencils printed here. Trace and cut them out as before.

2 Make sure the area you are planning to use is clean and dry and then, using a soft pencil, draw a rectangle measuring 2ft x 1ft 2in (60 x 20cm) where you want your floor mat to be.

3 Start with the checked stencil and butt it against the masking tape to make sure it is straight. Secure it firmly in place with the masking tape, stencil it in blue, as before, and leave to dry. Continue this process until the pencil area is filled with even blue checks.

4 Using the narrow masking tape, mask off the yellow border surrounding the blue checked square and stencil in yellow. Leave to dry and remove masking tape. Repeat this process using the jade green. Both borders line up with the checked area, leaving spaces in the corners for the corner motif.

5 Make a final border in blue using the same masking tape, this forms a complete rectangle that surrounds the design, and leave to dry.

6 Use spray mount to secure the corner stencils in place and stencil the corner motifs with the bronze wood dye.

7 Stencil the border design, round the outer edge in red, and leave to dry. Finally, spray mount the tassel fringe stencil in position along the two shorter outside edges and stencil with deep blue wood dye.

8 When the mat is dry, seal the mat with three coats of hard wearing floor varnish.

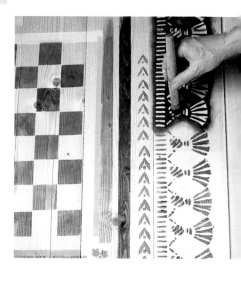

Bedroom makeover

This crisp lilac checked fabric, which I managed to buy inexpensively from a fabric warehouse, conjures up a summery country feel for this bedroom makeover and counterbalances the expense of the busy floral fabric I used for the borders.

BEDCOVER AND VALANCE

You will need

Checked fabric
Floral fabric cut into strips
Lining
Interlining
Scissors
Sewing machine
Needle and thread

1 Cut the check fabric into two pieces measuring 8ft x 6ft 6in (2.44 x 1.98m). Avoid making a centre seam by cutting one length of fabric in half length-ways and with right sides facing, join one of these pieces to one of each side of the main piece.

2 Cut four strips of floral fabric to edge the cover. Mitre the corners and turn in a ½in (1.5cm) turning along the inside raw edges. Pin and tack to the main body of the cover and topstitch in place.

3 Make up a piece of lining the same size and slipstitch it to the interlining. Place the main cover on the lining with right sides facing and pin, tack and seam around all the sides, leaving a gap big enough to turn the cover the right way out. Turn the cover out, press and slipstitch to close.

4 For the valance, measure from the top of the bed base to the floor adding 1½in (4cm) seam allowances all round. Double the length of the bed, and add the width measurement to work out the finished length of the valance frill. Multiply this figure by two and cut strips of the floral fabric to make up the amount required, adding an extra hem allowance of 4in (8cm).

5 With right sides facing, join the strips along the short ends and press the seams open. Hem the two raw edges at either end of the frill with a ½in (1.5cm) seam. Make two turnings along the lower edge and topstitch and run a line of gathering tape along the top of this piece ½in (1cm) from the edge.

6 Make up a piece of fabric to the same width and length as the bed, add a ½in (1.5cm) seam allowance and finish one short edge with a ½in (1.5cm) hem.

7 With right sides facing, pin and tack the frill to the raw edges of the flat bed piece, arranging the gathers neatly. Tack and machine stitch in place.

BEDHEAD

You will need

Two box cushions measuring
1ft 6in x 1ft 6in x 6in
(76 x 76x 15cm)
Terylene medium weight wadding
Checked fabric
Flower fabric
Shelf and pole to fit the length of
the bed
Scissors
Sewing machine
Needle and thread

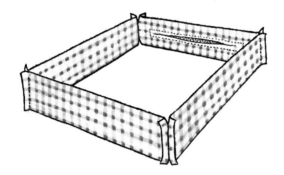
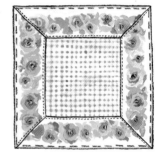

Cushions tied to a combined shelf and pole are hard to beat as a substitute for bedside tables. Wall hung lamps on swivel arms are an important part of this treatment as ordinary lamps require fairly deep shelves to sit on safely.

1 Cut out the front, back and three side pieces for the cushion covers and add a ½in (1.5cm) seam allowance all the way round. Cut a fourth side piece to the same length, adding 2in (5cm) to the width, and cut this in half lengthways.

2 Fold both cut edges 1in (2.5cm) under to the wrong side, and pin, tack and seam the zip to join the two pieces.

3 Cut out four ties 3 x 1ft 4in (8 x 10cm), fold them in half lengthways, with right sides facing, and sew round two sides with a ½in (1cm) seam, leaving one short end open. Trim the seams, clip the corners, and turn out and press. Following Diagram 1, pin and tack two to the top edge of the cushion front and two to the top edge of the cushion back.

4 Following Illustration 2, with right sides facing place the short ends of the side pieces together and sew to form a square.

5 Following Diagram 3, cut four floral stripes to fit around the cushion fronts. Mitre the corners and turn the raw edges under. Place on the front panel and pin and tack along the outside edges. Topstitch along the inner edges by machine.

6 With right sides facing, pin the top cushion cover to the side pieces. Open out the corners of

the side seams, tack all four sides to the top piece and seam. Pin and stitch the bottom cover to the side pieces, with right sides facing, leaving the zip open and seam together. Turn the right way round and press.

7 Cover the foam cushions with terylene wadding and slipstitch loosely to hold. Insert these into the cushion covers and zip them together. Tie the cushions onto the pole.

CIRCULAR TABLECLOTH

You will need

Check fabric
Rosy fabric
Lining fabric
Piping cord
Pencil
String
Drawing pin
Scissors
Sewing machine
Needle and thread

1 Measure the table diameter and add the length of the over-hangs plus a 1in (2.5cm) seam allowance. Add the measurements together and make up a square of fabric to the same size. If you need to join the fabric, centre a width and attach extra strips to either side to avoid a centre join.

2 Fold the fabric square into four, attach one end of the string to the folded corner using the drawing pin and tie the other end of the string to the pencil. Mark off a quarter circle and cut along the pencil line.

3 Repeat Steps 1 and 2 using the lining fabric. Place the cloth and lining with right sides facing and seam together around the circle, leaving a gap for turning the cloth the right way out. Clip the seam allowance with V shapes making sure not to clip the seam itself. Turn the right way out and press.

4 Make the frilled top using the method described for the valance (*see page 114*). You should however, make up the fabric piping first to sandwich between the top table top cover

and the frill. The frill should be 8in (20cm) deep and instead of cutting a rectangle you should, of course, cut a circle for the main body.

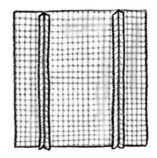

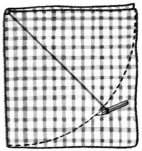

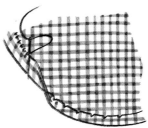

Trompe l'oeil table

Originally a plain Medium Density Fibreboard (MDF) shape this table uses colour photocopies of playing cards to create a fun trompe l'oeil effect of a game in progress. It combines a colour wash, edge decoupage and a cracked, ageing effect making a wonderfully stylish and original piece of furniture.

You will need

Blue-grey woodwash
Dark-blue woodwash
Fine tape, ¼in (5mm) wide
Masking tape
Paint brush
Craft knife
Artist's watercolour paintbrush
PVA glue
Medium grade steel wool
Artist's oil paint in raw umber
Scissors
Colour photocopies of cards
White spirit
Clean cloth
Base and top coat crackle varnish
Shellac

This look can be created using a variety of authentic traditional colours that are growing in popularity once again. It is important to use good quality colour photocopies of the cards, so insist on good quality paper as poor papers will buckle under the crackle varnish.

1 Check that the table surface is smooth, clean and dry, and then paint with two coats of the blue-grey woodwash.

2 To create the fine dark paint lines on the table top and drawer front, sandwich the fine tape between two strips of the masking tape. Lift the fine tape away and use the artist's paint brush to paint in the narrow line in the dark-blue.

3 To mask the curved lines running up the legs, cut the masking tape in half lengthways with the craft knife and bend it gently to the shape you want, cut edge facing outwards, manufactured edge facing inwards.

4 Use the artist's paintbrush to paint in the lines in the darker blue and leave to dry. Lift off the masking tape and gently rub back the lines with wire wool to soften them.

5 Cut out the coloured photocopies of the cards, glue them to the table with the PVA glue and leave to dry.

6 Apply the crackle varnish base coat and leave to dry. Apply the crackle varnish top coat and

leave to dry. These two coats will react, causing fine cracks to appear. Rub the raw umber into the cracks and clean any excess away with a small amount of white spirit and a clean cloth (*see page 138*).

7 Finish with a coat of the Shellac.

Hand painted chest

This delicately hand painted imitation French nineteenth-century chest started life as an old oak chest of drawers. With clever use of layered stencils, a few strategic brush strokes and subtle shading, these ribbons and garlands of fruit are made to look hand painted.

You will need

White acrylic paint
Sandpaper
Tracing paper
Graph paper
Scissors
Drill
Drawer handles
Felt tip pen
Stencil card and craft knife
*   or bevelled-edged glass,*
*   acetate and hot pen*
Artist's acrylic paint in
*   yellow ochre,*
*   cadmium yellow, vermilion,*
*   crimson, mid-green,*
*   cobalt blue, phthalo green,*
*   ultramarine and*
*   titanium white*
Large old plate
Masking tape
Damp cloth
Dry cloth
Stencil brushes
Artist's oil brush
Artist's fine paintbrush
Paintbrush
Clear acrylic varnish

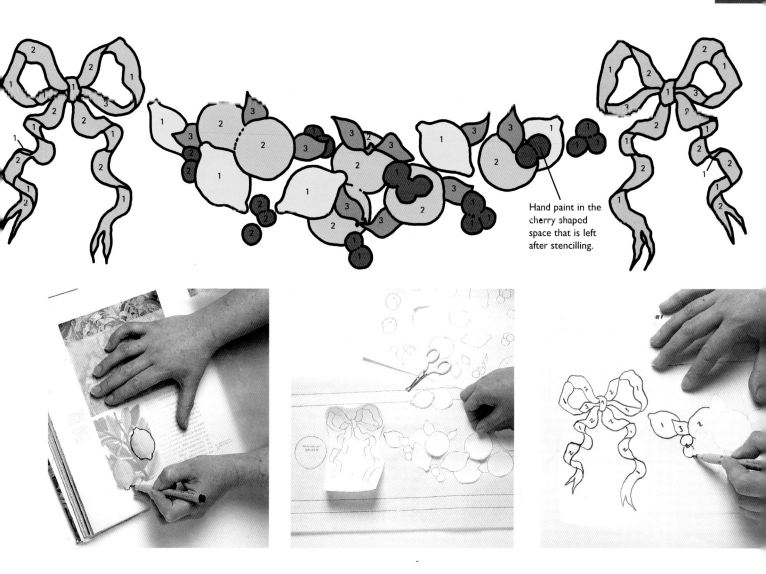

Hand paint in the cherry shaped space that is left after stencilling.

Having found this chest in a junk shop, I first removed the old handles and severe looking straight back and painted it in two coats of white acrylic paint. The trick to creating this hand-painted effect using layered stencils lies in the application of watery layers of thin colour that are wiped away almost instantly, in contrast to thicker pastel shades normally used in stencilling. The process does not require a high level of artistic expertise, just a steady hand and a lot of patience.

1 I traced these lemons, oranges, cherries, leaves and ribbons from a design source book I found in the library. You can make your own design in this way or trace the one printed here using a felt tip pen. Photocopy the tracing paper and cut out the individual shapes. The advantage of using tracing paper is that you can reverse the images, especially useful when it comes to the ribbons.

2 Cut out a piece of graph paper the same size as your drawer front. Mark the position of the bevelled edges and the handles. Using the photocopied cutouts,

arrange the fruit and leaves to create a garland between drawer handles, allowing room for the ribbons at both ends.

3 In this method of stencilling the shapes are butted directly onto each other and, in order to do this, you need to separate the images into three layers of stencils. Where one shape touches another, the stencils must be numbered differently and placed on a different stencil. See, for instance, how each adjoining twist in the ribbon design is numbered differently. Following these rules, number each shape on a master tracing, bearing in mind

you can have several colours on one stencil. For this design the first stencil contains lemons, some cherries and the bulk of the ribbon; the second stencil contains oranges and some twists of ribbon; and the third stencil contains leaves and two small pieces of ribbon. The shapes of the two cherries on the right hand side of the pattern will remain uncut.

4 Using sheets of acetate cut out the three stencils with a hot knife according to the numbers (*see page 72*).

 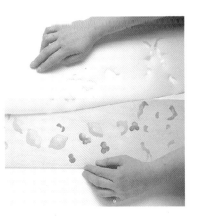  

5 Squeeze one blob of each colour of the acrylic paint onto the old plate. Mix the yellow ochre and mid-green paints with a little water and using the paint brush apply a thin layer of the mixture to the drawer fronts so that the white shows through. Work quickly as the paint will dry fast, and draw the paint towards the outside edges, making them slightly darker in colour.

6 Position your first stencil and secure it firmly with masking tape. Thin the cadmium yellow paint with water and then, using a dry stencil brush, fill in the shapes of the lemons. Immediately, before the paint dries, wipe away some of the paint at the top of the lemons to suggest highlights. The cloth must be damp, not wet, and the brush really dry or the paint will creep beneath the stencil. For extra depth add some shading to

the base of the lemons using the yellow ochre paint mixed with a little water. Next, stencil the cherries using a mixture of the cadmium red paint and a little water. Create highlights on the cherries, as you did for the lemons, using a damp cloth and shade them with the crimson and ultramarine paint. Use the dry cloth to clean the colours off the stencil brushes.

7 Continue this stencilling process, watering down all colours first, using blue and green for the bows with a touch of cobalt and titanium white. Gradate the colour so it is darker towards the outer edges.

8 Having completed the first stencil, place the second on top and line it up carefully. Stencil in the oranges, mixing cadmium yellow and vermilion. For the second bow stencil, create a

lighter colour by adding white to your original mix. Again wipe out highlights with the damp cloth.

9 Position your final stencil, and colour the leaves in a mid-green and water mixture. Wipe out the highlights and shade with concentrated paint towards the base. Stencil in the remaining ribbon pieces, highlighting and shading as before.

10 To shade the completed stencil, using a mixture of mid-green, cobalt blue paint and water, outline the bottom edges of the stencilled shapes with the fine artist's brush. Next, using a damp stencil brush, pull the paint outwards and distribute it evenly. Always keep a damp cloth at hand so that if you are unsure about the shading you can quickly wipe it away. Always start with a thin layer of paint, leave it to dry and apply more if

you need to later. By working this way, you will achieve a greater richness and depth of colour. The shadows should fall between and below the pieces of fruit. Leave a gap between the shadows that echoes the line and shape of the ribbons.

11 Apply a spot of white paint to highlight each image, including the twists in the ribbon with the small paintbrush. Smudge with a finger to soften. Wipe

away any excess paint with a damp cloth.

12 Using the fine artist's brush trace around some outlines of the ribbon, paint a line along the middle of each leaf and paint in the cherry stalks.

13 Using the paintbrush, apply a light layer of mid-green in a scrubbing action over the whole work, and immediately wipe off highlights on the fruit. This may

seem to threaten the delicacy of your work but, in fact, it will only serve to antique and soften it. Stipple the top and side bevelled edges of the chest in a mixture of the phthalo green, cobalt blue, titanium white and acrylic glaze. Protect with two or three coats of clear acrylic varnish and screw the drawer handles in position.

Country dresser

With the help of a few carefully shaped bits of wood and a scuffed peeling paint effect, this open shelf unit was dramatically transformed into a country dresser, making it the ideal piece of furniture for any country kitchen.

You will need

Skirting board measuring 6ft x 6in (2m x 15cm) to encircle three sides of the base
Wooden cornice measuring 6ft x 6in (2m x 15cm) to encircle the top front and sides
Timber measuring 6ft x 3in x 1in (2m x 7.5cm x 2.5cm)
Plywood to make up a back and two sides
Pine shelf measuring 1in (2.5cm) thick to make up two doors
Wooden moulding measuring 1½in (4cm) thick to frame the doors
Door hinges
Wooden doorknobs
Thick card
Scissors
Wood glue
Panel pins
Saw
Hammer
Jigsaw
Wood filler

You don't have to go to the expense of buying a pine shelf to create this country dresser as it is just as easy to transform any old and battered melamine or wood veneer bookcase that you might happen to have already at home.

1 Panel pin the plywood side and back pieces to the open shelf unit.

2 Cut the skirting board to fit the back, front and two sides of the base and mitre the ends at a 45° angle.

3 Cut a piece of card to the width of the skirting board and half its length. Following the pattern show, transfer the curved shape onto the cardboard and cut out a template. Lay the template onto the skirting board and trace around it using the pencil. Use the jigsaw to cut along the pencil line.

4 Glue and pin the skirting board in place. If the uprights to the unit stand proud, as they do here, cut a piece of wood to fill the space between uprights.

5 Repeat Step 3 and cut two decorative shelf edge shapes out of the timber and panel pin them into position within the uprights. Make sure that these are the same thickness as the uprights of the shelf, as they sit flush within them and butt onto the top edge of the shelf.

6 Cut three pieces of cornice, two for the sides and one for the front, and mitre the corners. Glue and pin them in place.

7 Cut the shelf board to make up two cupboard doors, sand down the rough edges and screw the hinges in place. Mitre the wooden moulding to create pan-

els for the doors, glue in place and attach the wooden door knobs. Fill any notches in the wood with filler and leave to dry.

8 Paint the cupboard in a colour of your choice and apply a peeling paint effect (*see page 144*).

Kitchen revamp

Of all the rooms in the house, the kitchen often takes the worst bashing. If you yearn for a new look for your kitchen which does not involve a completely new paint job and colour scheme, this colourwashing and decorated masking tape trick might be just the quick and easy solution you need.

You will need

Masking tape in a width that fits the recessed mouldings of your units
Hardboard measuring 5 x 2ft (1.52m x 60cm)
Off-white oil based eggshell paint
Blue oil based eggshell paint
White spirit
Metal ruler
Craft knife
Oil based clear matte varnish
Sandpaper
Medium paintbrush
Artist's paintbrush
Plastic pots

Like all the best decorating tricks this method of colouring masking tape to look like inlaid stone is simplicity itself. The secret is to use oil based paints mixed with some turps to prevent the tape from bubbling. If the kitchen doors are not too worn they may only need cleaning up with a scouring pad or you can apply a colourwash in a slightly deeper tone of the existing colour (*see page 135*).

1 Work out how much decorated tape you will need to edge the cupboard doors.

2 Make sure the hardboard is clean, dry and dust free. Stick the pieces of tape to the hardboard, butting them edge to edge as close as possible but not quite touching. Cover the board completely with the tape.

3 Add some turps to the off-white eggshell paint, one part turps to one part paint. Apply one coat of paint to the masking tape and leave overnight to dry.

4 Add some turps to the blue eggshell oil based paint, one part turps to one part paint, and paint over the masking tape.

5 Tear off a square of sandpaper measuring 5 x 5in (13 x 13cm) and, while the paint is still wet, comb the paint at a 45° degree angle using the manufactured edge to create a diagonal striped pattern in the paint. Leave the masking tape stuck to the board to dry overnight.

6 Lift a piece of masking tape off the board and stick it around the recessed mouldings on the cupboard unit door. As you work take care to mitre the corners by letting the two tapes overlap each other to form a cross. Press firmly with the metal ruler at a 45° angle over the tapes and use the craft knife to score a line across both tapes. Lift off the excess ends, and lay the two cut edges carefully side by side to form a perfect join.

7 If you need to join two tapes along the straight, allow them to overlap, lay the metal rule over both tapes at a 45° angle following the line of the striped paint effect and cut through both tapes with the craft knife. Lift both ends and tear the unwanted bits away very gently, and carefully lay cut edges side by side to form a perfect join.

8 If some of the painted tape does get torn away, you can retouch in blue using the artist's brush. Leave any touched up areas to dry thoroughly.

9 When you have completed all the doors and panels, apply a coat of oil based matte varnish to protect them.

Garden bench sofa

Even the cheapest sofa in the shops can make a huge hole in your furnishing budget. I devised this sofa, made from a small garden bench with fabric covers and soft cushions, to provide a convenient stopgap.

You will need

Tartan fabric measuring
15ft x 54in (5 x 1.37m)
Lining fabric measuring
6ft x 54in (3 x 1.37m)
Terylene wadding measuring
3ft (90cm)
Tracing paper
Felt tip pen
Medium size piping cord
measuring 21ft (9m)
Two zips, 20in (51cm)
Two box cushion pads measuring
20 x 20in (51 x 51cm)
Two back cushion pads measuring
20in x 20in (51 x 51cm)
Two bolsters measuring
1ft 6in x 6in (46 x 15cm)
Eyelet kit
Scissors
Sewing machine
Needle and thread

This striking tartan sofa was intended for a study but you, of course, can experiment with fabric prints and textures to create any look you desire. You will, of course, need to adapt the pattern and cushion sizes to fit your own garden seat. Good quality box cushions are an excellent standby and can always be adapted to provide extra seating areas for low level cupboards or a divan. While the zips on the box cushion covers may prove quite a challenge for some sewers, the back cushions are made to an easy envelope pattern and are a brilliant first project for any novice.

box pleats

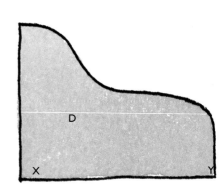

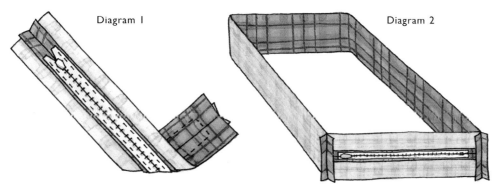

Diagram 1

Diagram 2

1 Measure the drop from the seat to the floor and the seat width and length. Following the pattern cut a piece of fabric to fit Shape A adding 1in (2.5cm) all the way round for seam allowances. The area within the dotted lines on the drawing represents the surface area of the seat.

2 Cut two pieces of the main fabric to fit Shape B for the back and front skirt and two pieces of the main fabric and the lining fabric to fit Shape C for the side skirts. Cut four 8in (20cm) wide box pleats to fit the seat to floor drop and eight strips measuring 1ft 3in x 2in (38 x 5cm) for the ties.

3 For the box cushions, cut four squares of the main fabric measuring 1ft 7in x 1ft 7in (48 x 48cm), two strips measuring 4ft 9in x 4in (1.45m x 10cm) and two strips measuring 1ft 7in x 6in (48 x 15cm).

4 For the bolsters, cut two pieces of the main fabric measuring 1ft 7in x 1ft 9in (48 x 53cm) and for the ends cut two circles of the main fabric measuring 7in (18cm) in diameter.

5 Hold the tracing paper against the side of the bench, mark out the shape with the felt tip pen and cut this out to use as a pattern. Cut four bench armchair side pieces to fit Shape D and two 3in (7.5cm) wide gusset pieces to fit along the outside curved edge.

6 Cover the bias binding with 2in (5cm) wide diagonal strips of fabric, joining on the diagonal where necessary. Lay the skirt pieces on their lining pieces, with right sides facing, and seam around three sides. Turn the right way out and press. Pin, tack and hem the inside corners of the main seat, Shape A, clipping the corners as shown on the cutting pattern.

7 Seam the skirt pieces, two B and two C, to the main seat cover, with right sides facing, sandwiching the bias binding in between. End the bias binding 4in (10cm) short of the end of the skirts, and make sure the raw edge of the bias binding is tucked in on itself. Fold back the sides of each skirt piece along the dotted lines, press and slipstitch them to the back of the skirt pieces.

8 With right sides facing, join the side arms to the gusset along the curved edges, make two turns along the back and bottom raw edges and pin, tack and topstitch in place. Make an eyelet hole in the top of the gusset. Repeat for other arm. Cut and make up four 12in (30cm) ties and sew onto the side arms at the bottom two corners marked X and Y.

9 To make up the box cushions, cut the shortest gusset piece in half lengthways and fold back a 1in (2.5cm) turn along the cut edge. Following Diagram 1, pin, tack and seam the zip between the folded edges. Following Diagram 2, with right sides facing pin the longer gusset piece to either end of the short gusset and press along the corner lines. Following Diagram 3, pin and tack the top and bottom pieces of the cushion to the gusset pieces, with right sides facing, sandwiching the covered piping in between and clipping the corners before seaming through all the layers. Turn the right way out and repeat for the second box cushion.

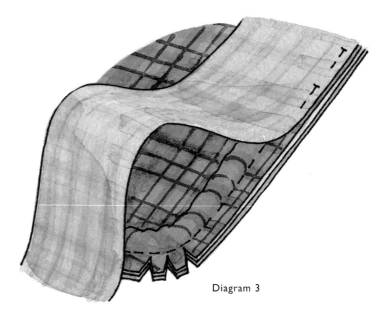

Diagram 3

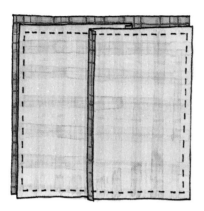

Diagram 4

10 Following Diagram 4 make the back cushions by cutting two pieces of the main fabric measuring 20 x 20in (51x 51cm) and four pieces 1ft 1in x 1ft 8in (33 x 51cm). Make two folds down the longest sides of the smaller pieces and pin, tack and hem. These should butt onto each other if you lay the pieces flat with right sides up.

11 With right sides facing, lay the largest piece flat, and then place the other two pieces on top, overlapping the hemmed edges. Seam along all four sides, turn the right way out and press.

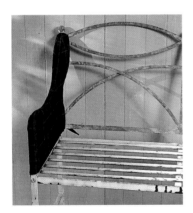

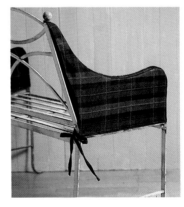

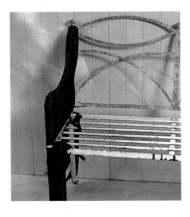

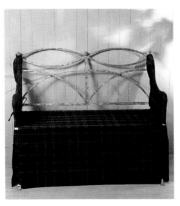

12 To assemble the sofa, tie the four box pleats to cover the corners of the bench. If your bench has not got slats, you can screw eye hooks into the underside of the seat to slot ties through. Place the side arms in place, and slot the top eyelet over the protruding metal screw, having first removed the ball top, and secure the ties. Place the box seat cushions, back cushions and side bolsters in position.

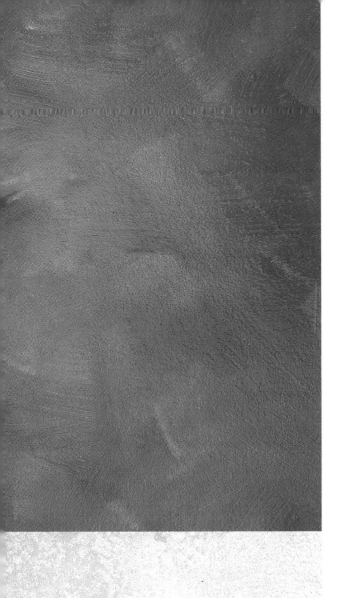

Painting magic

With so many decorative paint effects now being packaged in easy to use pre-tinted glazes and kits, the promise of turning walls into silk moiré, or old furniture into family heirlooms is hard to resist. For those still experimenting, here are some of the easiest paint effects and antiquing tricks.

Sponging off

Sponging off creates a regular, one colour, nearly opaque effect as you start with the advantage of an even coat of glaze which you apply first with a brush and then lift it off with a sponge revealing the base colour below. You can work in several colours and here I mixed two glazes, the first a soft sea green and the second a sharp mint green. I didn't wait for the glaze to dry between applications, but you can vary the look by sponging off one colour and then leaving it to dry before repeating the process with the next glaze.

You will need

Vinyl silk paint for the walls
Natural sponge
Acrylic glaze
Artist's acrylic paint
Paintbrush
Water
Card
Acrylic varnish
Plastic pots

1 First, paint the walls with a coat of the vinyl silk paint. Once that is dry mix the glazes following the directions on the tin. Most acrylic glazes are designed to be mixed with one part paint colour and six parts of glaze, with some having an open time of up to an hour but this can vary. Work over small areas of the wall at one time since glaze dries quickly.

2 Apply the first glaze (sea green) with the paintbrush, covering wall surface evenly. While the first coat is still wet apply the second glaze (mint green), again making sure the surface is evenly covered.

3 Soak the sponge in water and wring it out. Dab it evenly on to the tinted glaze using a quick light movement. Change the direction of your wrist as you work to vary the effect and avoid repeats in the texture. Be careful not to swirl the sponge or you will create cloudy streaks. When the sponge becomes saturated with the glaze, rinse it in clean water. The more glaze that you remove, the lighter the finish will be.

4 To get into the corners of a room, hold a piece of card to protect the adjoining wall and to dab into the corners using a narrow edge of the sponge.

5 If you are unhappy with any uneven patches, wait until the glaze is dry, and then lightly sponge extra glaze onto areas that are too light, and use the basecoat to dab at patches which look too dark.

6 In hardwearing areas of the home such as the kitchen and hallway, apply a protective coat of acrylic varnish.

Colourwashing

Colourwashing is simple to do and produces a fresh opaque finish. As a paint effect it is particularly suited to uneven walls, where it helps to disguise flaws and imperfections that ordinary paintwork would show up and it makes a perfect background to stencilling. Here I have chosen to apply a purple wash over a blue ground using broad random brush strokes. For a gentler finished effect you can wipe off the glaze with a cotton rag and apply a single colour when this has dried.

You will need

Off-white vinyl silk basecoat
Paintbrush, 4 in (10 cm)
Acrylic glaze
*Artist's acrylic paint in
    ultramarine, purple
    and white*
Dry cotton rag
Card
Acrylic varnish
Plastic pots

1 Seal the surface of your wall with a coating of the off-white vinyl silk paint and leave to dry. Mix one part of ultramarine to one part white of the artist's acrylic paint and six parts glaze. Then mix the purple glaze in the same way. If you are intending to decorate a complete room it is important to mix all your glazes at one time, as it is impossible to mix exactly the same colour twice.

2 Test a small patch of the blue glaze on the wall. If it looks too heavy, wipe it off with a damp cloth and dilute it with water for a lighter effect. Brush on the blue glaze in large criss-cross strokes over an area of about 2–3 sq ft (1 sq m). Brush out the glaze thinly and evenly; depending on the temperature of the room, you should have an open time of about one hour.

3 When the first coat has dried, apply a coat of purple glaze in the same way, covering any gaps and breaking up any dark patches.

4 Stand back from your work to assess it. The final effect should be soft and cloudy, so any dark, heavy patches can be removed at this stage, while the glaze is still wet, with a cotton rag. Wipe the rag over the brush strokes in a circular rubbing action.

5 If you want to create a more intense effect, mix up the blue paint and glaze as before, but omit the white paint. Wait for the walls to dry and then apply the stronger colour. If the effect is too dark, wait for the walls to dry, mix a soft thin white glaze, and brush it over the entire surface to knock it back. The advantage of colourwashing is that as it is such a quick process, you can always apply a second, third or fourth colour, until you are completely satisfied with the results.

6 Continue working until you have completed the room. To brush into the corners use the card to mask the adjoining wall.

7 Apply a final coat of protective acrylic varnish in rooms vulnerable to wear and tear.

Dragging

Dragging is one of the more traditional looking paint effects that originally developed from wood graining techniques. This soft striped finish looks formal and elegant on walls, furniture and doors. Dragging is not difficult, but requires a steady hand and a special dragging brush, which has longer bristles than usual. As with all paint techniques, the results vary according to the colours you use. To counteract an over harsh striped effect, choose a basecoat and top glaze in colours which tone rather than contrast. You can practise on a small area of wall for a first attempt, and wipe off the glaze while it is wet and start again.

You will need

Off-white vinyl silk paint
Paintbrush
Dragging brush
Traditional green pre-tinted glaze
Plumb line
Masking tape
Polythene sheeting
Acrylic varnish

1 First, paint the walls with a coat of vinyl silk paint. Once that is dry, mix the glaze following the directions on the tin. For this I used a traditional green pre-tinted glaze that you could mix yourself using clear glaze and artist's acrylic paints in mid-green, ultramarine and yellow ochre (*see page 138*).

2 Protect the skirting board, picture rail, ceiling coving and ceiling with masking tape and polythene sheets. This is important as you will need to continue dragging the brush past the area you are covering. Apply a thin coat of the glaze from floor to ceiling in bands measuring about 3ft (1m) wide.

3 Draw the dragging brush from the top to the bottom of the walls using an even pressure and keeping the strokes parallel. To guarantee a tidy top edge, butt the brush against picture rail, or ceiling cove, and press the bristles gently against the wall with the other hand, making a definite line of contact before pulling the brush downwards.

4 To ensure the brush marks remain straight, hang a plumb line slightly ahead of your work to use as a guide. If you need to use a ladder, you can lift off the brush halfway down the wall, and when you resume work, repeat the last 1ft (30cm) of the stroke you just completed. This should help you to avoid creat-

ing join marks. To make sure that you have a tidy bottom edge, extend the brush stroke over the skirting board protected in polythene. Wipe the brush clean with the cotton rag at regular intervals to stop it from becoming overloaded with glaze.

5 Continue working in 3ft (1m) bands and aim to finish the whole room in one session. If this is not possible, make sure to break along a corner edge and make sure you have enough glaze mixed for the whole room.

6 Protect the finished work with a coat of acrylic varnish, especially in household areas subject to wear and tear.

Ragging

Ragging is a popular technique as it does not require any special tools and results in a soft, sophisticated and consistent finish, rather like crushed velvet, that is easy to achieve. You can vary the finish according to the type of rag you use. Old cotton sheeting is perfect for a neat finish, whereas old towelling or chamois leather will produce a rougher texture. As you work, the rags become saturated with glaze and will have to be replaced, so make sure you have enough on hand to tackle a whole room.

You will need

Off-white vinyl silk paint
Pretinted acrylic glaze
Paintbrush
Stippling brush
Cotton squares measuring
*   20 x 20in (51 x 51 cm)*
Acrylic varnish

1 First, paint the walls with a coat of the off-white vinyl silk paint. Once that is dry, mix the glaze following the instructions on the tin. For this effect I used a pretinted coral clear glaze. Starting in the corner of the room, paint a thin and even coat of glaze onto the walls, using criss-cross strokes and working in 3ft (1m) sections.

2 Stipple the area to break up the brush strokes, using a stiff paintbrush or a stippling brush with a short, sharp, hammering action. To create a plain ragged effect, dab randomly with a round shaped crumpled rag, twisting your wrist as you dab over the work to avoid repetitive textures. Try crushing the fabric and releasing it a couple of times before you bunch it up for use as

this gives the final finish a more interesting texture.

3 When the rag is covered with the glaze, refold it to expose a clean, dry spot and when it becomes oversaturated with the glaze, replace it with a new one. To rag the corners of a room, make a small tight bunch of cloth, and press carefully into the edge of the wall without touching the adjoining surface. If the adjoining wall is wet, protect it with a piece of card.

4 Once you have finished one strip, stand back to evaluate the results, and half close your eyes. If there are any dark patches, dab them a second time with the rag. Continue this process until you have finished the room. Protect the finished work with varnish, especially necessary in areas exposed to wear and tear.

Ageing and distressing

Over the years decorators have refined various techniques for simulating the character of antique furniture. The challenge lies in recreating the beauty of an old polished surface, as well as cracks and signs of wear and tear that give antique furniture its mellowed, faded glory and historical appeal. When applying these techniques to new wood, on the whole historical and traditional colours work better than bright clean modern colours, but do bear in mind it is easier to knock back and mellow a bright surface with dark wax than to revitalize one that looks too dark. Here are some of my favourite techniques. It is always worth testing various small samples before tackling a larger piece of furniture.

**PEELED OR
CRACKLED PAINT**

You will need

*Water based vinyl silk paint in
    dark-green, aquamarine and
    bright-blue
Peeling paint medium
Clear acrylic varnish
Artist's acrylic paint in burnt
    umber
Paintbrush
Plastic pots*

This is sometimes referred to as crackle glaze but it is, in fact, a medium resembling a milky varnish that is designed to be applied between two coats of different coloured vinyl silk paint. It will begin to craze almost as soon as the top coat of paint is applied and when dry, it can be rubbed over with raw umber, a ready prepared antiquing paint or a patenting varnish. I used this method and this particular combination of colours for the country dresser transformation (*see page 127*).

1 Apply a water based vinyl silk paint in dark green and leave the piece to dry.

2 Apply a generous, even coat of the peeling paint medium, working in one direction and avoiding drips or runs. Leave the piece to dry again.

3 Apply the second coat of aquamarine vinyl silk paint with a generously loaded brush and apply boldly and evenly in one direction. The cracks show up best under thick layers of paint, so as you work make sure that you do not overbrush and as soon as the paint begins to look thin make sure to reload your brush. An uneven pattern of cracks will begin to appear almost immediately, the unpredictable nature of this effect adding to its authenticity.

4 Mix the bright blue paint with equal quantities of water, apply a coat of this solution and leave to dry.

5 If you want to mellow the colour, rub burnt umber into the cracks and it will turn olive green.

6 Finally, apply a coat of acrylic varnish and leave to dry.

CRACKLE VARNISH OR CRAQUELURE

You will need

Vinyl silk paint
Crackle varnish kit
Small paintbrushes
Artist's oil paint in raw umber
White spirit
Soft cotton cloth
Polyurethane varnish

Crackle varnish, or craquelure, is sold in kits of two varnishes. The oil based varnish is applied first and then a fast drying water based varnish reacts with this and causes the surface to craze. The cracks are highlighted either with gilt cream, gilt powder or raw umber paint that is rubbed into the cracks when the varnish is dry. It is possible to vary the size of the cracks by delaying the application of the second coat of varnish.

For large cracks

1 Apply a thin and even coat of the oil based varnish over the vinyl silk paint base.

2 While the varnish is still slightly tacky, apply a coat of the water based varnish. Allow to dry until cracks appear.

3 Using the paint straight from the tube, rub a blob of oil based raw umber into the cracks with a soft cotton cloth. Immediately remove any excess with white spirit.

4 When this has dried, apply a coat of polyurethane varnish as the water based varnish can easily flake away in time.

For small cracks

1 Apply a thin and even coat of the oil based varnish over the vinyl silk paint base. Leave to dry.

2 Apply a second even coat of the water based varnish over the entire surface of the base coat. As the varnish is transparent, it is not always easy to see which areas have been covered. The trick is to angle the surface and let the light show up the wet patches. Leave the second coat to dry forming tiny cracks. Repeat Steps 3 and 4 as before.

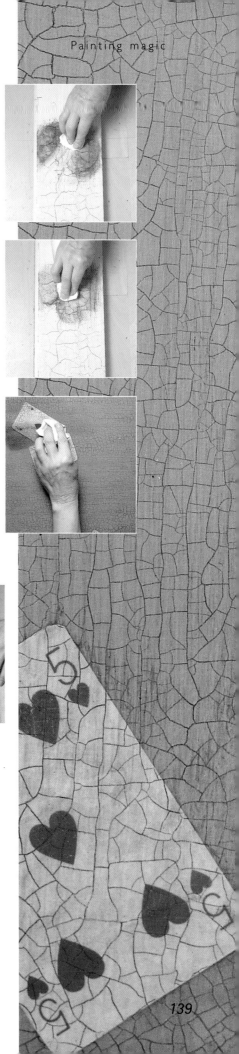

DISTRESSING WOOD WITH PAINT LAYERS

You will need

Earth brown and dark-green vinyl silk paint
Steel wool
Paintbrush
Beeswax polish
Soft cloth
Plastic pots

This technique can be applied to both new and old wood. New wood can benefit from a coat of mid-brown varnish, but if you are using darker colours it is not always strictly necessary.

1 Apply a vinyl silk basecoat in earth brown emulsion and leave to dry.

2 Apply a coat of dark green vinyl silk paint and leave to dry.

3 Using the steel wool, rub back the top coat in patches to reveal the first layer of vinyl silk and, in some places, to reveal the wood grain.

4 Apply a fine wax paste polish and, using a soft cloth, rub to a soft sheen.

Easy marbling

Natural marble comes in so many colours and patterns that it is not surprising there are many different versions of marble paint effects and several ways of achieving them. The most popular imitation marble effect is a white Carrara Italian marble, often used for fireplace surrounds, panelling and table tops. There are three stages to marbling, first painting an eggshell oil based basecoat under a layer of oil glaze, second, distressing the glaze and finally, painting or feathering veins. All this must be done in one session while the glaze is wet. Although you can use water based paints for marbling, oil based paints allow a longer working or open time and often look more convincing. Take care when working with oil based paint and dispose of waste paint in a plastic bag filled with sand. Real marble is usually cut into manageable stone sizes and used in panels (see page 106). As with most paint effects, always experiment first on a scrap of board. It is useful to have a sample of real marble or a photograph to refer to.

You will need

*Off-white oil based eggshell
    paint*
Clear oil glaze
Artist's oil paint in black
Stippling brush
Softening brush 3in (7.5cm)
Large feather
Cotton cloth
Small artist's paintbrush
White spirit
Oil based polyurethane varnish

1 Apply two coats of the off-white eggshell paint allowing it to dry between coats. Mix five tablespoons of glaze, five tablespoons of eggshell off-white and half a teaspoon of the black artist's oil paint with a little white spirit. Apply a thin coat of this mixture, using criss-cross strokes, to your surface.

2 Break up the brush strokes with the stippling brush. Add another half a teaspoon of the black artist's oil paint, mixed with white spirit, to the grey glaze

mixture. Apply a series of long diagonal wiggly lines in the new dark grey paint while the background glaze is still wet, trying to avoid creating parallel lines.

3 Remove some of the solid colour between and along the grey lines by gently wiping the cloth in a wiggly line.

4 If any of the grey areas look too solid, take a corner of the cloth and drag it over the surface of the paint, blurring the edges with a softening brush.

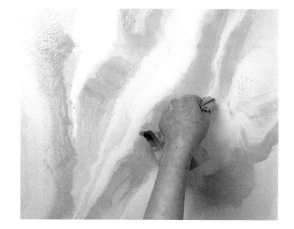

5 Add a quarter of a teaspoon of the black artist's oil paint, mixed with white spirit, to the remaining grey glaze mixture.

6 Draw the edge of the feather through the paint and apply wiggly diagonal lines along the join where the grey areas meet the white ones; the veins should look like tributaries of a river. Use the softening brush again to break up the lines.

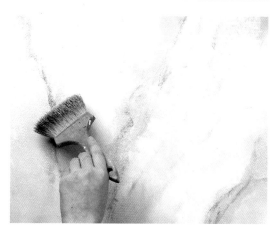

7 Tap the artist's brush, loaded with white spirit, against a piece of wood held in your other hand to create small pale craters of white spirit in the paint. Do not overload the brush or the white spirit will run. Quickly apply the softening brush to stop the craters from spreading.

8 When the glaze is dry, apply a coat of varnish for protection and also to give the surface a solid sheen like real marble.

Index

Acknowledgements

I could not have put this book together without my kind and understanding husband Andrew, who starved when I was up against deadlines, and my sons Harry and Robert who helped with the word processing. The Lord knows, that above all, I thank Him for all His inspiration, ideas and for putting talented people in my path who generously shared extra tips and techniques.

I am indebted to Terence Whelan, former editor of *Ideal Home* who suggested I wrote this book in the first place, and to Sally Gillam and Liz Keevill at *Ideal Home* who painstakingly edited text alongside Katie Cowan at Hamlyn. I am also grateful to Richard Madeley and Judy Finnigan who gave me vital popular feedback on much of the content of this book when I worked with them on *This Morning* at Granada Television.

I am so thankful for the many paint effects courses I have been invited to attend at The Stencil Store, Paint Magic and Relics of Witney, and the people in charge who inspired me: Mick Flynn, Lyn Thorpe, Selina Khara, Sara Delafield Cook, Elaine Green, Pam Corder and Brett Wiles. Thanks to the set builder, Roger Egleton, for his expert help and advice on all the projects involving carpentry. Thanks also to Pat Isted and Sandy MacCaw who helped make up my fabric ideas and to Eileen Foreman who helped me with typing. I am thankful also to Sarah Spooner, one of the leading designers at Colefax and Fowler with whom I was fortunate enough to give joint lectures, and who taught me many useful top professional tricks.

Most of the photographs in the book where taken by Di Lewis, who magically filled them with sunshine even on grey days and worked at a remarkable pace.

The companies listed below loaned and supplied products for the projects to make this book look beautiful and for their help I am especially grateful.

A.S. Handover Dutch metal leaf 72–73, 96–97; **Allens** stair ballusters 96–97; **Artisan** curtain rods 14–15; **Avante Garden** furniture 14–15, 106–107; **B.H.S.** lamp 106–107; **Brewers of Putney** paint 26–127; **Celia Birtwell** voile 20–21; **Christy** towels 58–59; **Colefax and Fowler** upholstery fabric 82–83; **Complete Stencillor** hot pen 44–45, 72–73; **The Curtain Mill** fabric 18–19, moiré 34–35, lilac check 114–117; **The Decorative Arts Co. Ltd.** waste paper basket 22–23, mirrors and paint 72–73; **Designers Guild**, fabric 14–15, 60–61, 92–93, 114–117; **Divani** sofa 22–23, 86–87; **Dormy House** blanket box 58–59, screen 78–79, 106–107; **Dulux paints** 106–107; **Elaine Green** stencils 10–11, 84–85; **The English Stamp Company** 52–53; **Eric Sharpe Paper Marble** table design 102–104, technique 126–127; **Farrow & Ball** paint 66–67; **French Linen Company** linen 36–37; **Glorafillia** tapestry pictures 114–117; **G.P.& Baker** fabrics 16–17, 40–41, wallpaper 38–39; **Graham and Green** accessories 12–13, 34–35; **Grange** table 60–61; **Habitat** chair throws 8–19, chairs 42–43; **Harrison Drape** curtain pole 86–87; **Ikea** open shelf unit 124–125; **Integra** curtain pole 20–21; **The Isle Mill** fabric 128–129; **Jab** curtain fabric 82–83, silk tartan 128–129; **Jali Products** pelmet 70–71, brackets 80–81, 84–85; **Jane Churchill** fabric 54–55, 118–119; **John Lewis** lampbase 22–23, lamp 86–87, fabric 46–47; **Laura Ashley** voile 36–37; **Liberon** liming wax 38–39, 98–99, wood dye 98–99; **London Shutter Company**, shutters 8–9; **Lyn Le Grice** bee stencil 54–55, tree stencil 78–79; **Marston Langinger** wire furniture 64–65; **Monkwell** fabric 12–13, 70–71; **Next** voile 8–9; **Nicola Wingate Saul Print Room** decoupage 68–69, 106–107; **Offray** ribbons 26–27, 42–43; **Osborne & Little** fabrics and wallpaper 14–15; and fabrics and ringing 64–65; **Oxley Furniture** chairs 102–104; **Paint Magic** stencils 10–11, paints 88–89, 94–95, frames 98–99, paints and decorative effects 118–119, paints, glazes and crackle varnish 134–141, projects 88–89, 118–119; **Pam Corder** layered stencils 120–124; **Penelope Kennedy** wrapping paper used on walls 8–9; **The Pier** chair 70–71, 124–125; **Polyvine** frosting varnish 10–11, glaze 80–81, paints, glazes and crackle varnish 134–141; **Ratcliffes** glazes 102–104; **Relics of Witney** Annie Sloane's paint 10–11, 42–43, paints, glazes and crackle varnish 134–141, Colourman paints 84–85; **Rhode Designs** chest 88–89; **Romo** fabric 58–59, 76–77; **Ronseal** paint and grain kit 108–109, wood dyes and varnishes 110–111, coloured wood dyes 112–113; **Sandersons** fabrics 24–25, 38–39, 44–45, 52–53, 86–87, 34–35; **Scumble Goosie** table 118–119; **The Stencil Library** ribbon stencil 78–79, stencils 112–113; **The Stencil Store** stencils 10–11, star stencil 54–55, paints and glazes 78–79, 82–83, verdigree kit 84–85, paints and crackle varnish 124–125, paints, glazes and crackle varnish 134–141; **Tom's Flowers** pots 124–125; **Trade 80** silk 92–93, fabric 102–104; **W.H. Newson** louvres 78–79; **Windsor & Newton** artists colours 102–104, paints 120–124; **Winther Browne** wood mouldings 10–11, mouldings 42–43, 108–109, carvings 76–77; **Woolpit Interiors** lamp 40–41.

The publishers would also like to thank the following people for supplying photographs for this book

Di Lewis and Maggie Colvin 16–17, 18–19, 40–41 top left, 42–43, 44–45; **IPC/Robert Harding Syndication/Ideal Home/Malcolm Robertson** 1 top detail, 1 middle detail, 4–5 bottom middle, 6 top right, 26–27, 28–29 top left, 28–29 top centre, 34–35, 40–41 bottom right, 46–47, 68–69, 74–75 bottom left, 80–81, 92–93 bottom left, 92–93; 132–133, 134–135, 136–137, 140–141; **IPC/Robert Harding Syndication/Ideal Home/Di Lewis** 2 detail, 4–5 top left, 4–5 middle left, 4–5 bottom left, 4–5 top centre, middle centre, 6 left, 6 top centre, 6 bottom, 8–9; 10–11, 20–21, 23 inset picture, 24–25, 28–29 right, 28–29 bottom centre, 30–31, 32–33, 36–37, 40–41 left, 40–41 top centre, 40–41 bottom centre, 40–41 centre, 52–55, 54–55 top right, 54–55 top centre, 54–55 middle centre, 54–55 middle right, 56–57, 64–65, 66–67, 70–71, 72–73, 74–75 top right, 76–77, 78–79, 84–85, 86–87 inset picture, 92–93 top left, 92–93 bottom centre, 98–99, 100–101 bottom left, 102–105, 120–121; **IPC/Robert Harding Syndication/Ideal Home/Dominic Blackmore** 100–101, 114–117; **Ronseal/Mike Good** 108–109, 110–111 main picture, 112–113 main picture; **Octopus Publishing Group Limited/Di Lewis** 1 bottom detail, 2 main picture, 4–5 top right, 12–13, 14–15, 22 steps, 23 main picture, 28–29 bottom right, 38–39, 54–55 right, 54–55 bottom left, 58–59, 60–63, 74–75 top left, 74–75 bottom right, 74–75 bottom centre, 82–83, 86–87 main picture, 88–89, 92–93 top centre, 92–93 right, 94–95, 96–97, 100–101 top, 100–101 bottom right, 110–113 steps, 118–119, 120–123, 124–125, 126–127, 128–131, 138–139.